AN *Elephants* IDEA

A BASIC COMPANION FOR WRITERS

MIKA Q. SHIPLEY

Kendall Hunt
publishing company

Cover images © James G. and Elizabeth R. Troutman.

Kendall Hunt
publishing company

www.kendallhunt.com
Send all inquiries to:
4050 Westmark Drive
Dubuque, IA 52004-1840

Copyright © 2014 by Kendall Hunt Publishing Company

ISBN 978-1-4652-4446-8

Printed in the United States of America
10 9 8 7 6 5 4 3 2 1

CONTENTS

PREFACE

The premise for this textbook is that those of us who were raised surrounded by the English language understand how to use the language, especially in speaking. However, many of us, for whatever reason, simply have forgotten the "rules" of grammar. And "the elephant in the room" is the fact that many of us feel ill-equipped when we are called upon to write.

As you might know, elephants never forget. For this reason, I chose an elephant to be used on the cover of this textbook. The elephants that appear in this textbook are located at the David Sheldrick Wildlife Trust Elephant Orphanage in Nairobi, Kenya.

Here is the website for it, if you want to learn more: http://www.sheldrickwildlifetrust.org/about_us.asp

Africa will be one of the reoccurring themes throughout this textbook. I hope you enjoy it as much as I enjoy sharing it with you!

ACKNOWLEDGMENTS

I want to thank the contributors for this text, including Kevin M. Brien, Bo Burnham, Rick Detorie, Jennifer Kalita, Christie P. Lassen, Stephan Pastis, Carissa Scaniffe, Garry Trudeau, and the editors at the *Ocean Pines Independent* and *The Maryland Coast Dispatch*. A special thank you is sent to my good friend and talented artist Maggie Steimer. My sincere thanks go to my production team at Kendall Hunt Publishing Company, including Lauren Vondra, Sheri A. Hosek, and Taylor Hunsberger.

I appreciate the support from my colleagues and many students at Wesley College, especially Sarah Bullock and Joncara Marshall. I also want to acknowledge my past teachers and mentors who still inspire me, especially Dr. Joseph L. McCaleb and Dr. Shirley Wilson Logan at the University of Maryland, College Park.

I received so much encouragement from my friends, including Holly Otto Bennett, Nadine Bernard, Debbie Gabriel, Shelley Hoffman, Richard and Cheyenne Huettel, Jane Keller, Steve and Kim Meek, Harriet K. Oliver, George and Beth Schoolfield, and George and Anna Vitek.

Finally, I am deeply appreciative to my family for their love and encouragement, my brother J.C. Troutman, my niece Pennie J. Troutman, my parents Fay and George Spangler and Jim and Liza Troutman, who took the fantastic Africa photos, and my understanding and loving husband, Matthew.

ABOUT THE AUTHOR

Dr. Mika Q. Shipley (formerly Troutman) received her Bachelor's degree in English from the University of Delaware in Newark, Delaware. She spent many years in banking before returning to her goal of teaching college writing. She earned her Master's degree in writing from Towson University in Towson, Maryland, in 1999. At that time, she started teaching writing courses at Towson University and York College of Pennsylvania. She earned her Ph.D. at the University of Maryland, College Park, Maryland, in 2003. After completing her doctoral degree, she taught at Loyola University of Maryland in Baltimore, Maryland, until 2006.

Dr. Shipley is now an Associate Professor of English and the writing program director at Wesley College in Dover, Delaware, where she has been teaching since 2006. She lives near Ocean City, Maryland, on the Atlantic coast with her husband, Matt, and their cat, Sammie. In addition to teaching and writing, Dr. Shipley enjoys traveling, cooking new and often strange recipes, and socializing with friends.

CHAPTER 1
Choices

© 2014 Digital Storm. Used under license from Shutterstock, Inc

Congratulations on choosing to explore writing at the college level. The key to your success is that you chose to begin this journey. If you feel like you are being forced to read this text or take this course, your success could be less than what you hope to achieve.

Writing is tough work. It requires a great deal of critical thinking and patience. If you have an open mind and are willing to work hard, you are sure to see improvements in your writing. And, maybe, you'll learn a little bit about yourself in the process.

THE WRITING SITUATION

One of the first tasks you might be asked to do is to respond to a question in writing. This should not be difficult; you have choices.

For instance, you might be asked the following question:

Who are you? What is your experience in writing thus far?

In high school, you could parrot back, "I am so and so and my experience with writing is …"

What you should consider is your **purpose**. All writers have an aim. They strive to accomplish that aim or purpose by considering to whom they are writing, their **audience**, and for what **occasion** they are writing for. You see? You can even end a sentence with a preposition, as I just did (despite what you've been told). Other than earning a letter grade, you have other purposes. You could even discover yourself by writing. You could reevaluate the way you think about yourself as a person and a writer. Try to forget what you have been told in the past about your writing. You have a new beginning.

Consider the following purposes:

To analyze

To classify

To define (in your own words)

To describe

To narrate (tell a story)

To propose a solution

To explain

To evaluate

To illustrate

To compare and contrast

To market yourself, someone, or some idea (to persuade)

To take a position about an issue

Rarely do writers have just one purpose. For instance, if you want to be considered for a particular job position, you will have to describe your experience and education and you will have to persuade the employer that you are the best person for the job.

Consider that your audience has a particular need to be fulfilled, and you are fulfilling that need. You need to get a certain point across and how to go about it is difficult at best. Simply put, write in a manner that makes you feel the most comfortable. You might be just learning how to write at the college level, and your professor is here to help you.

Your reader is your friend and you should not be afraid of being criticized. Every word is a precious commodity. Lots of writers are worried about word count.

Don't count words; count ideas! Sophisticated writing comes from sophisticated thought or vice versa. Consider the following prompt.

Prompt 1.1

Your professor has asked you to describe in a paragraph of 200 words or less, why you have come to college.

Now you might be more concerned about word count than what you actually have to write. But you should not be. Consider your purpose and your audience. You came to college because you want to better yourself in some way, so describe this. Word counts are often arbitrarily applied. You probably already realize that sometimes paragraphs are quite lengthy, and sometimes they are not. In fact, you can have a paragraph that consists of only one sentence.

EXPECTATIONS OF STUDENTS VS. EXPECTATIONS OF COLLEGE PROFESSORS

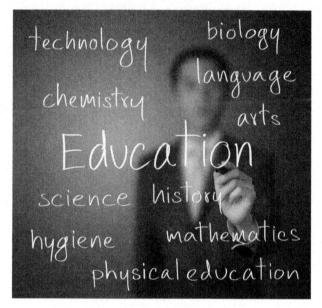

© 2014 Dusit. Used under license from Shutterstock, Inc.

College professors have many assumptions or beliefs about the expectations they have for their students. Alternately, college students expect many things from their college experience. When these expectations match, an ideal situation occurs. However, unfortunately, this is not always the case. Consider the following prompt.

Prompt 1.2

1. What is your sense of how college is different than high school?
    A. Academically:

B.   Socially:

Your expectations probably come from many sources: older siblings, parents, teachers, advisors, and the real myth-maker—the media. You probably are quite aware of some of these myths about college that are portrayed in movies and on television.

Prompt 1.3

List all the ways college is portrayed in the media.

Your professors will probably have many conversations with you, either individually or as a class, about their expectations. Here are just some of these expectations that apply specifically to your writing class:

○   Your writing professors have the time and will take the time to read your writing thoroughly.

○   You are expected to attend every writing class. Your writing class will be interactive including class discussions and workshops. Unlike high school, college courses vary depending on the subject of the course.

○   You will write a lot both in class and outside of class.

○   You will discover that most of the time, procrastination will not be your friend when it comes to your writing class.

○   Your writing professors care about your learning, first and foremost; they have little tolerance for interferences from your personal life and any lack of responsibility.

SURVEY OF ACADEMIC WRITING EXPERIENCES

1. During high school, or if you have taken college courses, what kind of writing assignments have you had? What successes have you achieved? What challenges have you faced?

2. What is your sense of how college-level writing is different from high school?

3. What experiences have you had with writing workshops or peer review?

4. What experiences have you had with writing as a process (brainstorming, drafting, revising, and editing)?

COMMONLY CONFUSED WORDS

We hear and speak words without any thought to how they are spelled. In writing, spelling matters, and we are all extremely lucky to have spell-check in most of the technology we use. But, as you may know, spell-check does **not** catch every misspelled word, and sometimes it can even change your intended word to something else entirely.

Consider the following example:

> Shelley definitely had time to shower after the gym.
>
> Shelley defiantly had time to shower after the gym.

Definitely and *defiantly* are spelled differently, pronounced differently, and have entirely two different meanings. When typing on your keyboard, you might easily accept the spell-check software's suggestion for your intended word, as in the example above. I once had a student in my Business Writing class who intended to write "veterinarian assistant" on her résumé for one of her past part-time jobs, and instead, she wrote "vegetarian assistant." She certainly would have been embarrassed if she had sent out the draft of that résumé to a potential employer.

Words are confused all the time. In this section, just some of these commonly confused words will be reviewed. As a writer, you want to be aware of the ones that you seem to often have problems with. Words can be confused with other words for three main reasons:

1. They are **homonyms**, or words that sound alike but are spelled differently, such as *hole* and *whole*.

2. They are pronounced in the same way (by some speakers depending on their backgrounds) but they are spelled differently, such as *are* and *our*.

3. They are just plain confusing, like *affect* and *effect*.

The following poem was written by Bo Burnham a comedian, songwriter, and actor. You might know him from the MTV series *Zach Stone Is Gonna Be Famous*, a 2013 mockumentary that Bo wrote, directed, and starred in. This poem appears in Bo's book, *Egghead or, You Can't Survive on Ideas Alone.*

"Homonyms"

Homonyms aren't fare.

It's awful. It's tragic.

I say I'm pulling out my hare

and they think I'm talking magic.

© 2014 Photo Africa. Used under license from Shutterstock, Inc.

Careful writers know that using a dictionary, proofreading slowly, and developing an understanding of the words that cause the greatest personal difficulty are the best strategies for avoiding these errors.

a part / apart

a part: These are two separate words referring to a piece or a portion of something.

My new computer desk was missing a part.

apart: As one word, this means separately in relation to another or another position.

I can never tell the twins apart.

advice / advise

advice: This is an opinion about a course of action.

My best advice for you is to complete your general education credits first.

advise: This is a verb to offer advice or a recommendation.

I advise you to complete your general education credits first.

affect / effect

affect: This is a verb meaning to cause change or to influence.

Smoking can greatly affect your health.

effect: Most of the time this is a noun meaning a result of something.

Some of the health effects of smoking are lung cancer and heart disease.

HINT: To remember the difference between the two words, consider "the effect" with the "e" ending "the" and starting "effect." "Affect" would never take the article "the."

aisle / isle

aisle: This is a narrow hallway.

    The faculty formed a line in the auditorium's center aisle.

isle: This is a small island.

    The sailboat circled the isle in the northern bay.

are / our

are: This is a form of the verb "to be."

    We are ready to leave when you are.

our: This is a plural pronoun showing possession.

    We could not locate our dog anywhere in the park.

assure / ensure / insure

assure and ensure: Both of these verbs mean to make certain.

    The lawyer will ensure his client will be at the courthouse tomorrow.

    He assured the judge.

insure: This verb means to cover by insurance.

    Paul will have to see about insuring his baseball bat with the Hall of Fame players' signatures on it.

conscience / conscious

conscience: This refers to our conduct or ethics.

    She could not cheat on her boyfriend and keep a clear conscience.

conscious: This refers to being fully aware or awake.

    The paramedic checked to make sure the victim was conscious.

freshman / freshmen

freshman: This word refers to a single first-year student **or** describes a word following it.

    The freshman could not find the location of the freshman orientation.

freshmen: This word refers to two or more first-year students.

    The auditorium could barely hold the 200 freshmen.

NOTE: Increasingly, "first-year students" is replacing "freshmen" due to the perceived sexism of "freshman," similarly to "fireman" and "mailman."

have / of

The confusing nature of these two words stems from speaking phrases like "should have," "would have," or "could have," as in the following sentence:

    My brother should have been home by now.

Many speakers say something that sounds like "should of," but this is written "should have."

its / it's

its: This is a pronoun showing possession.

That cat likes to chase its tail for hours.

it's: This is the contraction of "it is."

I was told that the mall's entrance is on the south side. It's not there.

loose / lose

loose: This describes something as not tight or not secure.

His loose change was in the front pocket of his loose jeans.

lose: This is a verb meaning to be unable to find something, to misplace something, or to fail at something.

He tries really hard not to lose his temper.

passed / past

passed: This is the past tense of the verb "to pass."

She passed the final exam easily.

past: This describes something that happened at an earlier time.

Her lack of time management skills is past history.

principal / principle

principal: This refers to the head of a school or an organization or describes the main part of something.

Olivia always runs into her elementary school principal at the grocery store.

HINT: You might remember the hint "the principal" (ending in "pal") is your "pal" in order to remind yourself of this definition.

George could not forget the principal reason for his boss's decision.

principle: This refers to a set of beliefs.

Anna always follows the principle of honesty first and foremost.

sight / site / cite

sight: This is one of our senses, the ability to see.

site: This is a location, especially now on the Internet, as in a website.

cite: This is a verb meaning the use of a source that you quote or paraphrase.

suppose / supposed

The confusing nature of these two words stems from speaking as well; we don't hear the "d" in "supposed."

suppose: This means to assume or to consider possible.

I suppose I will try to make it to your party Saturday night.

supposed: This is the past tense of "suppose" and means intended.

I was supposed to go to your party last Saturday night.

than / then

than: This word is used for comparisons.

This winter has been colder than any I can remember.

then: This means at a particular time or next in time.

Matt will wash the dishes and then take out the trash.

their / there / they're

their: This is a pronoun showing plural possession.

The students could not locate their classroom in the new building.

there: This means at a specific place.

Your car keys are right there where you left them.

they're: This is the contraction for "they are."

They're concerned about their son's behavior.

though / through / threw

though: This means the same as "although."

Richard wanted to buy earrings for his wife even though he could not afford them.

through: This means to go from one side to another.

Now that I cleaned the windows, I can see through them.

threw: This is the past tense of the verb "to throw," meaning to toss.

The team won the game when Brandon threw the ball to home base.

to / too / two

to: This means to go toward some place or person, or it is used in a verb form, like "to have."

Sharon could not wait to give her gift to Pennie.

too: This means the same as "also" or "very."

I am too tired to go to the midnight study hour.

two: The second number after one.

Eric billed his client two hundred dollars.

use / used

use: This means to put in service.

I use my favorite coffee mug every day.

used: This is the past tense of the verb "use," or as in the expression "used to," it means having been or done before.

I used to have a cleaner kitchen when I used the dishwasher daily.

vary / very

vary: This verb is used to describe change.

I will try to vary my sentence length.

very: This adverb is used to mean extremely or truly.

I am very sorry for your loss.

weather / whether

weather: This refers to the conditions outside, and there is always some sort of weather.

NO: I wonder if we are going to get any weather today.

YES: I wonder if we are going to get any stormy weather today.

whether: This is used to show a possibility.

I wonder whether we are going to have storms today.

who's / whose

who's: This is the contraction of "who is."

Maria voted for Carlos who's the most popular sophomore.

whose: This pronoun shows possession.

Jeremy is the friend whose car I borrowed.

your / you're

your: This pronoun shows possession.

Your basset hound really needs to go to the vet.

you're: This is the contraction of "you are."

You're going to be in deep trouble when you get home.

EXERCISE 1.1—Confusing Words

Underline or highlight the errors you find with word use. Then revise them.

According to the American Diabetes Association (ADA) approximately 26 million Americans suffer from the <u>affects</u> *effects* of type 1 or type 2 diabetes. Fortunately <u>they're</u> *there* are many ways to keep the disease under control. Loosing weight is a great way to control symptoms of the disease. Additionally, for those managing diabetes who are <u>use</u> *used* to testing there blood sugar, many gadgets now exist for home testing. Diabetes patients should keep track of their blood sugar levels in order to notice changes over hours, days, and weeks. This way they can report to their doctors if their levels are higher or lower then passed testing. The emotional state of diabetes sufferers is especially important; diabetes patients should talk to their doctor if they experience depression for longer than to weeks. There doctors can advice them about appropriate therapies.

Exercise not only helps to lower blood sugar levels, but it can aid in weight loss and good heart health. Some diabetes patients have made a <u>conscience</u> *conscious* decision to work out threw the <u>workweek</u> as apart of their normal schedules. Nutrition is also a key factor in managing diabetes. Moderation and balance are the two principals that keep patients within their recommended number of carbs. Having diabetes does not mean giving up everything that could of caused the diabetes in the first place.

CHAPTER 2

Focus

Photo courtesy of James G. and Elizabeth R. Troutman.

READING ACTIVELY

It might seem odd to have "reading" in the beginning of a "writing" book, but our literacies are shaped by both reading and writing. As you have already realized, unlike high school, you are expected to buy your own textbooks, **and** you are expected to read them. There are differing levels of how much reading you will be expected to complete for different college courses. Some professors use the textbook as the primary form of instruction for a course. Others will assign reading but never discuss the reading in class. Then when it comes to an exam, the exam will have questions from classroom activities and lectures and the reading. Do not make the assumption that if your professor never discusses the reading in class, then you are not expected to be responsible for the reading.

You might have had a teacher in the past who would assign reading for homework, and then in a class after the homework assignment, the teacher would tell you every important point about what you read. In this scenario, students figure out quite quickly that they don't need to do the reading. Their teacher will tell them about all the important information from the reading they assigned.

Rarely does this happen in college. You will be expected to complete all reading even if it is never discussed in class. For this reason, you need to read actively for understanding—what is called reading comprehension. How do you do this? Here are some ideas that might help you.

When reading for your college courses, you should consider what you are reading in the context of the specific course. The reading you complete for your anatomy course will be quite different than the reading you do in a literature course. I often hear students complain that reading is boring. A few years ago, I asked a student whom I advised and who was in danger of failing out why he didn't crack open a single textbook. He said, "I just couldn't get into it. Reading is boring." Some textbook reading can be "boring"; however, your learning is **not** the same as your being entertained.

When approaching a reading assignment, have a positive attitude and try to create an interest in some aspect of the material. Sure playing video games might be more interesting, but the reading will only add to your learning and success in college.

Much has been said about the millennial generation not reading anymore. With technology being what it is, reading is occurring, but in a different format. You might be reading more and more on computer screens than an older generation could only imagine. Whatever format you are reading, you must maintain focus. When you set out to read for a course, give yourself a quiet environment with little distractions. Your level of comprehension will be much higher, and you will probably read more quickly than you would if you try to read in a noisy atmosphere with too many distractions.

To prompt active reading, preview the material by looking at titles, headings, pictures, graphics, and other side features. This will possibly pique your curiosity about the content of the material contained in the reading. Try to form a few questions that this previewing has already raised in your mind. You can even write these in your course notebook or in the textbook's margins. Then, make it your goal to have your reading answer these questions.

Even if you are renting your textbook instead of purchasing it outright, you have permission to write in it. This will not alter your rental agreement, nor will it affect how much you can sell the book for if you intend to do so at the end of the semester. I encourage you to read with a pen in your hand. You can continue to write questions that you hope the reading will answer. You can underline keywords and ideas that you want to review more later. You can also mark words or ideas that you need more information on, or are confusing to you. Any vocabulary that you do not understand should be marked, so you can consult a dictionary. If you don't understand the words, chances are you don't understand the reading, or worse yet, you misunderstand the reading. When you take notes while reading, you are annotating your reading. Making notes about your reading will help you when you go back to review the material.

Be careful about highlighting. I have seen too many students who highlight vast quantities of their textbook. This might be a symptom of a short attention span. These students could be highlighting their reading and actually postponing their reading comprehension.

Don't skip over graphics like pictures and tables. You are responsible for understanding the graphics too, and they often hold valuable information in addition to the words that you read.

Break up your reading into manageable units of time. No one can read for eight straight hours and retain much of anything. Consider your time schedule and your own reading speed, and plan out your reading times.

When you have finished a reading session, give yourself a few minutes to reflect on what you read. You might even want to write a short summary of what you read. Write down more notes about the reading, along with notes about where you are in your reading and what you have left. Do you still have unanswered questions? Write these down. This annotation will make it easier for you when you return to the material.

Finally, you might want to get a reading buddy from the same class, so you can talk about the reading. Talking about the reading will help you retain the information. You can also help each other if one of you misunderstands something or one of you "zoned out" during a reading session.

"Civility in the Networked Age" by Valerie J. Gross

The following article draws a connection between the use of technology and communication among the different generations. Valerie J. Gross is the president and CEO of the Howard County Library System in Maryland. The article originally appeared in *The Baltimore Sun* on October 6, 2013.

Prompt 2.1

Gross opens her article with questions to get you thinking about her topic. Take a minute to answer these three questions before reading the rest of the article.

CIVILITY IN THE NETWORKED AGE

by Valerie J. Gross

How many times per day do you check email and texts? How quickly do you expect a response? What about Facebook and Twitter? 1

In an infomal survey conducted by the Howard County Library System (HCLS) this summer, answers ranged from "500 times per day" to "never." It's likely no surprise that millennials (18 to 30) checked the most frequently, while baby boomers and members of the Greatest Generation (those of us who are 50 years old and "better"—and who still send an occasional birthday card via snail mail) checked the least. 2

Teens represent the leading edge of connectivity. Their use of technology often signals future changes in the adult population. Those of us 50-plus will therefore likely continue to increase our total smartphone glances per day and may even eventually switch to Facebook birthday greetings. 3

Although technology clearly adds convenience to our daily routines, we may be fooling ourselves into thinking that the quality of our relationships with our work colleagues, friends and loved ones has improved. We would like to believe that our smartphones, with which many of us are now inextricably linked, strengthen our connections with others as we "like" Facebook postings and respond immediately to texts. Yet this may not always be the case.   4

To illustrate, picture the following restaurant scene. Two lunch companions sit across from each other eating lunch "together." Neither is talking (or eating for that matter). Neither looks at the other. Cocooned in their own texting worlds, their eyes focus downward on their iPhones.   5

I smile and shake my head, while my millennial son, who finds nothing odd about this scene, may not even hear my typical baby boomer comment as he concentrates on responding to an incoming text himself.   6

For parents, social networking presents a similar conundrum: how much communication is too much? While texting and online chatting allow parents and children to stay constantly up to date, children also need to learn how to operate independently. Among parents who have a child between the ages of 12 and 17, two-thirds use one or more social networking sites. in 2011, 80 percent of parent social media users whose children were also users of social media had friended their child on the sites. The increased ability of "helicopter parents" to hover over their children's every move via social media alters the development of these relationships.   7

The experiences of the various living generations differ vastly, which affect our points of view and thus our behaviors and relationships. For example, I can remember when television meant NBC, CBS, and ABC, with all three off the air at midnight. My son knows only 24/7 access—to whatever he wants whenever he wants it. My world began without computers. My millennial son was born into the MySpace world, which then moved to Facebook (which now, brace yourself, has 1.15 billion users).   8

Given the prevalence and immediacy of technology and social media, have our ideals of civil behavior changed? Does a generational divide separate those who live and breathe new technology from those who use it to a lesser extent, if at all?   9

Facebook, Twitter, Tumblr, Pinterest, Yelp, Vine, Instagram and Snapchat have certainly altered the nature of our relationships. Facebook can reconnect us with long-lost friends and family members, and grandparents benefit immensely from Skype to form bonds with distant grandchildren. So in these ways, the immediacy of technology has improved our relationships.   10

At the same time, we no longer invest as much time connecting with others in person. The loss here is that only face to face communication, and also phone calls to an extent, afford us the opportunity to interact optimally, allowing us to respond to a verbal pause, puzzled look, questioning tone of voice, or smiling eyes. Also, hugs are not yet possible on Skype.   11

Missing over the Internet, these nuances assist in clear communication, minimizing miscommunications. In addition, when we speak in someone's presence, we temper our language, which we might not feel compelled to do when tapping on a screen or keyboard.   12

Indeed, the complexities of rapidly changing technology and social media require constant adaptation, affecting how we inter-relate.   13

CHECKING YOUR READING COMPREHENSION

Without looking back over the article, answer the following questions.

1. Provide one example of a difference between the author when she was young and her son.

2. According to the article, which generation checks e-mail the most frequently?

3. What is one benefit of technology and social media stated by the author?

4. According to the author, what is one reason face-to-face communication is the better form of communication?

REACTION TO WRITING

1. Gross's title is "Civility in the Networked Age." What is meant by the word *civility*?

2. If you do not know the meanings of the following words, try to determine their meaning from the surrounding context in Gross's article. Check their meanings in a dictionary and write a sentence using each word.

   inextricably (4)

   cocooned (5)

   conundrum (7)

prevalence (9)

optimally (11)

nuances (12)

temper (12)

3. Gross uses the term "helicopter parents." What does she mean by this term?

Prompt 2.2

In one paragraph, describe one or more drawbacks you have had with technology, social media, and communication.

Prompt 2.3

In one paragraph, describe your experience with "helicopter parents."

Prompt 2.4

In one paragraph, answer one of the two questions that the author asks in paragraph nine.

DIFFERENCES BETWEEN WRITING AND SPEAKING

One idea that is difficult for your writing professors to explain is how writing is different than speaking. In fact, this is one of the premises of this book: we speak quite fluently with our friends, family members, professors, and employers, but when it comes down to writing, we all have many challenges.

Consider the differences between writing and speaking. You probably think right away about having no body gestures (like moving our hands) and facial expressions. If you consider some not so evident differences, it might help you become a stronger writer.

We don't have to worry about spelling when we speak. This is the most obvious difference, and we're fortunate to have spell-check programs to help us, although we know they're not always reliable.

We don't have to worry about punctuation when we speak. In fact, much of what we say are incomplete sentences punctuated by pauses and sounds that are not really words, like "um."

We don't have to worry about "rules" of writing so much when we speak. Most of the time, our speaking is much less formal than what we have to write for a particular audience who we might fear will judge us.

We can't rely on some of our bad habits of speaking when we are writing. One example of this is the word "like." All of us probably know someone who inserts this word in *like* every other sentence. Other fillers that we use in speaking that we should avoid in writing include starting sentences with "Well" and "So."

ACADEMIC WRITING VS. NON-ACADEMIC WRITING

Just like writing is different than speaking, writing for college is different than writing for other scenarios like writing a note to your mom or writing a memo for work. I generally don't like to dictate rules to my students, but over the years, I have compiled the following list. Consider these suggestions for ALL writing for college. This includes homework, e-mails to your professors, and formal academic papers.

By all means, avoid the language that you use in your texting. Throughout the day, we move among many forms of communication: texting, speaking, listening, taking notes, and writing for college. Being aware of the changes that you must make for different forms of communication and for different audiences is the key to being successful in switching from one form to the next.

> NO: u jus dont get it lol

Similar to texting language, shortcuts like abbreviations (*etc.*) and slashes (*and/or*, *he/she*) should be avoided in academic writing.

Contractions like *can't*, *don't*, *shouldn't*, and *isn't* are difficult to avoid. Contractions are becoming more acceptable in academic writing, but my advice is to avoid overusing them. Some professors still find them unacceptable in formal writing.

Finally, slang should be avoided.

> NO: I mean don't get me wrong. I was just chillin with my dawgs. We were just hanging out.

PARTS OF SPEECH

Generally, there are considered to be seven parts of speech in the English language.

1. Nouns—refer to a person, place, thing, or concept. Proper nouns generally have capital letters like your first and last names and the name of a specific person, place, or thing. The underlined words in the following sentence are all nouns.

   <u>Anthony</u> makes his <u>mother's</u> favorite marinara <u>sauce</u> every <u>year</u> on her <u>birthday</u>.

2. Pronouns—take the place of a noun. *He, she, it, they, their,* and *your* are all pronouns.

3. Verbs—tell the action that is happening for the subject or link the subject to another word or words that describe it.

   Anthony <u>cooks</u> like a professional. (*cooks* describes the action of Anthony)

   Anthony <u>is</u> an excellent chef. (*is* links Anthony to the description of him)

Verbs have many tenses. For just two examples, present tense verbs describe actions happening right now (bring, catch, dance, forget), and past tense verbs describe actions that happened in the past (brought, caught, danced, forgot).

4. Adjectives—describe nouns and pronouns. These often answer the questions "What kind?" (*big*) "How many?" (*five*) and Which one(s)? (*those*).

    Those five big dogs all belong to my sister.

5. Adverbs—describe or modify verbs, adjectives, or other adverbs. These words often end in *–ly*, like *badly*. These words answer the questions "How?" "How much?" "Where?" "When?" "Why?" and "To what extent?"

    He <u>carefully</u> carried the baby. (answers "How?")

    He could hold the baby <u>forever</u>. (answers "To what extent?")

6. Prepositions—relate a noun, pronoun, or verb to another word and usually tell where something is, where something is going, or when something is happening.

    Christine was arrested <u>at</u> her job. (answers where she was arrested)

TABLE 2.1	Common Prepositions						
about	at	down	inside	off	over	throughout	up
above	before	during	into	on	past	to	upon
across	behind	except	like	onto	regarding	toward	with
after	below	for	near	out	round	under	within
along	between	from	next	out of	since	unlike	without
among	by	in	of	outside	through	until	

7. Conjunctions—connect words, phrases, and clauses to each other. A simple way to remember the main conjunctions is FANBOYS (for, and, nor, but, or, yet, so).

Many people have learned that articles and interjections are parts of speech also. Articles refer to the words *a*, *an*, and *the* used with nouns. Interjections are generally one word or an expression that shows emotion like *Oh!* *Hooray!* *Good grief!* Interjections often take exclamation points, or when used in a sentence, followed by a comma.

The parts of speech refer to the way a word works in a sentence. Many words can work as many different parts of speech.

For example, consider the following sentences:

Kimmie went for a twelve mile <u>run</u> with her dog Charlie.

Kimmie will <u>run</u> for twelve miles with her dog Charlie.

In the first sentence, *run* is a noun. In the second sentence, *run* is a verb.

Why do you need to know the parts of speech?

College educated adults need to know many specialized languages. Just think about all of the specialized language in science or psychology classes, like "frontal cortex." The same is true for your writing classes. You need to know the same language that your classmates and instructors use. This way when you hear or read a comment like "you should think about a stronger verb in that sentence," you will know exactly what the comment means.

EXERCISE 2.1—Parts of Speech

Write the part of speech of each underlined word on the corresponding numbered line.

We are fortunate to have such an <u>abundance</u>[1] of birds in North America. Most Americans appreciate <u>their</u>[2] neighborhood birds. However, these <u>same</u>[3] birds can be nuisances <u>daily</u>[4]. For instance, some neighborhoods, especially near lakes and ponds, have a <u>large</u>[5] population of Canadian geese. These geese often do not <u>migrate</u>[6] and can pollute parks <u>with</u>[7] their waste. <u>Many</u>[8] solutions exist to fix this problem, but often communities choose to try to relocate the birds, or worse yet, euthanize them. An ingenious idea to control the waste comes <u>from</u>[9] Toronto: the "poop" machine. This <u>machine</u>[10] <u>basically</u>[11] cleans away the goose poop. The parks <u>stay</u>[12] clean, and otherwise <u>happy</u>[13] communities can live in harmony with the geese.

_____

1 _____

2 _____

3 _____

4 _____

5 _____

6 _____

7 _____

8 _____

9 _____

10 _____

11 _____

12 _____

13 _____

Another bird that can cause damage is the woodpecker. Woodpeckers tend to stay in the same areas, and[14] they can wreak havoc for utility companies by pecking holes in[15] wooden utility poles. This has led[16] to high[17] costs for the industry with many wooden poles lasting only a few[18] years. Fortunately, another[19] solution to this particular bird problem exists: steel poles[20]. Steel poles can last decades and[21] stand up to the woodpeckers and other creatures that like[22] wood. In fact, people have reported[23] seeing woodpeckers pecking away on[24] steel poles without causing damage to the poles or themselves. With the increase use of steel poles, maybe woodpeckers will return to the trees in their territory, rather than pecking holes in costly[25] poles.

M. Steimer

————————

14 _____

15 _____

16 _____

17 _____

18 _____

19 _____

20 _____

21 _____

22 _____

23 _____

24 _____

25 _____

THE BASIC SENTENCE

We form sentences all the time without even thinking about it. If you look at a sentence in terms of the way it's made, it starts with a capital letter and ends with a period, question mark, or exclamation point. Sentences are also called independent clauses, meaning they can stand on their own.

Sentences must have a subject and a predicate in order to be considered complete.

SUBJECT   +   PREDICATE   =   SENTENCE or INDEPENDENT CLAUSE

A complete sentence can be only two words.

It snowed. *It* is the subject and *snowed* is the predicate.

Subjects

Subjects are usually nouns or pronouns, and they are doing something or are being described.

The smartphone is ringing.

In this simple sentence, the simple subject is *smartphone*. The predicate is *is ringing*. Subjects can also be compound, meaning more than one subject is connected by *and*, *or*, or *nor*.

The dogs, birds, and cats filled the entire lobby of the domestic animal museum.

Dogs, *birds*, and *cats* are the compound subjects of the sentence.

The complete subject refers to the simple subject (one word or more than one in the case of a compound subject) and all the words around it that modify it.

<u>The pure-bred dogs, exotic birds, and rare cats</u> filled the entire lobby of the domestic animal museum.

The underlined portion of the sentence is the complete compound subject.

BOX 2.1—Subjects

Simple Subject: only one word that is usually a noun or a pronoun.

Compound Subject: more than one subject connected with *and*, *or*, or *nor*.

Complete Subject: the simple or compound subject and all the words surrounding it that modify it.

Predicates

Predicates contain the verb of the sentence and show what is being done to the subject or what the subject is doing. In the same way as subjects, we can refer to the simple predicate, the compound predicate, and the complete predicate.

The smartphone <u>is ringing and vibrating frequently</u>.

The underlined portion of the sentence is the complete compound predicate.

EXERCISE 2.2—Subjects and Predicates

Use a slash / to separate the complete subjects from the complete predicates.

1. The "Freshman Fifteen" refers to the weight gain of at least fifteen pounds that many first-year college students experience.

2. Weight gain among both male and female college students can happen for many different reasons.

3. Often college students are faced with many unhealthy food choices like fast-food and junk food.

4. When students are busy with studying, participating in activities and sports, and socializing, they just grab the quickest, often unhealthy, food.

5. Another reason the "Freshman Fifteen" can creep up is late-night eating and/or drinking.

6. College students have the independence to stay up too late, indulging in all sorts of food and alcohol that are high in calories.

7. Inactivity and lack of exercise can lead to weigh gain also.

8. Sometimes first-year students come from a family-life where they are used to having home-cooked food served to them every day.

9. It is important that students learn to take care of themselves when they are away at college.

10. Getting a good night's sleep, making healthy food choices, drinking responsibly, and exercising regularly are great ways to keep off the unwanted pounds.

CHAPTER 3
Independence

"I know that I am intelligent because I know that I know nothing."

—Socrates

ADVICE FOR FIRST-YEAR COLLEGE STUDENTS

Over the years, I have collected advice from my writing students as they reflect on their first year in college. Here is a condensed list:

1. Don't be afraid to be yourself. Being different is okay; you'll be remembered for your individuality.

2. Go to the events at orientation. They may be corny, but they're a great way to meet people from all over campus.

3. Spend less time thinking about how others see you and more time thinking about how you see yourself.

4. Take advantage of free food whenever possible. Midnight breakfast is a great source of nutrition.

5. Don't try to be someone you're not when making new friends. Just be yourself and let it flow. You will have new friends in no time.

6. Don't have expectations for your college experience. When there are no expectations, you can't be disappointed. Just live your life and see where it takes you.

7. Don't forget your roots. Just because you're perfect in this moment doesn't mean your past didn't shape your life. Let the people from the past know you miss them.

8. Don't expect to be completely comfortable from the start. You have to step outside of your comfort zone. Home will always be there, but these new opportunities will not. Take advantage of them.

9. Get involved with other freshmen. The friends you make now will be like your family for the next four years, and hopefully longer.

10. Balance is key. Don't be all work and no play, or vice versa. Find your middle ground.

11. When you look around and all you see are happy faces, don't be fooled. Everyone is just as apprehensive as you are.

12. Befriend your Resident Assistants, for they will help you in the long run. Don't be quick to judge them; they are regular people too.

13. Do something outside of your comfort zone—it could end up being your passion.

14. Appreciate the friends you made before you came to college. They helped make you who you are. But don't let the memories of them prevent you from making new memories.

15. Never wait until the last minute to do your work. Procrastination is a terrible reason to waste your tuition payments.

16. Laugh. Do it often. It is one of the easiest means to escape reality and the best way to feel carefree.

17. Don't take yourself too seriously. You only have a few years left before doing something crazy becomes doing something immature.

18. Do not close the door to your dorm room. You never know who might come wandering through it.

19. Freshman year is over before you know it. Savor each moment. Even when a drunken stumbler wakes you up in the middle of the night. Trust me, someday you'll actually miss the noisy freshman dorms.

20. Form deep bonds and true friendships that will last an eternity. Smile, sing, dance, jump around, go streaking, eat exotic foods, play, cry until you have no more tears, laugh until it hurts, and celebrate life!

Prompt 3.1

When you review this list, which ones seem particularly meaningful to you?

Why?

NARRATION—REPORTING, DESCRIBING, AND TELLING YOUR STORY

In college, rarely will you be asked to narrate a story like the narrator does in any good story. However, you will be asked to provide many reports of something that happened. This reporting requires many skills:

The ability to reveal yourself—If a particular story is important to you then your readers will need to get a sense of why this story is important.

Attention to detail—You will have to describe important details, so your readers can recreate in their minds the story you recall.

Attention to chronological order—Generally, stories are told in the order that the events happened.

The Use of "I"

You might have been told that you can not use the first-person pronoun "I" in academic writing. This simply is not true. You will have many occasions to use "I" in your writing for college. When you are asked to report about something that happened to you, it's nearly impossible to avoid using "I."

That being said, there are also instances where the use of "I" is not permitted, for example in the sciences for certain types of reports. The important idea to remember is the writing situation: your audience, your purpose, and the occasion you're writing for. You need to evaluate the situation that you're writing for in order to decide whether to use "I." If you are unsure whether "I" is permitted for a particular assignment, then all you have to do is ask.

In addition to "I" being unacceptable for certain writing situations, another reason you might have learned that "I" is not permitted is to avoid constructions like "I think." Consider the following example.

A reporter for the Weather Channel says, "I think it will rain later today." Or the same reporter says, "It will rain later today."

Which is stronger—the first statement or the second? Chances are you chose the second. When you're writing, just like reporting in the example above, your reader knows what you write is what you think. Try to avoid statements like "I think," "I believe," and "I feel."

Chronological Order

When writers are reporting about an event that happened in the past, they typically use chronological order to describe what happened first, what happened next, and so on. This can be achieved by using transitions for time.

TABLE 3.1 Transitions for Time	
first, second, third	meanwhile
after, afterward	next
before	now
currently	since
during	soon
eventually	subsequently
finally	then
last	when
later	while

By permission of Rick Detorie and Creators Syndicate, Inc.

Creativity

I have had many students who claim they like creative writing, but they claim they are not good writers when it comes to non-creative writing or writing for school and work. I have also had students who want to make up stories about themselves when we start narration. I try to make students understand that there is definitely room for creativity in academic writing.

When we write, we are creating. We strive to be as fresh and original as possible. Yes, the writing you do for this class might seem non-creative; however, creativity is part of everything you write. You are writing your ideas to an audience who has not heard them before. Each writer brings his or her unique perspective to the writing situation.

Your role as a writer is to explain, but you also will invent. Every new thing you write is an invention, and creativity is a big part of that. You are writing prose for this class, and ultimately this prose takes the form of an essay or a paper. You are not writing short stories, poems, or song lyrics, but this is something you should continue to do. The more we write and the more we dabble in other genres or forms, we improve as writers.

When you are telling your story, I encourage you to be as honest as possible. Making up stories probably will cause you more problems in the long run. With that being said, I also encourage you to have some creativity in what you write for college. You should have the confidence to know that you have plenty of experiences to draw on, and you should express them confidently and creatively.

"And you cannot go on indefinitely being just an ordinary, decent egg. We must be hatched or go bad."

C.S. Lewis

NARRATION—AN EXAMPLE

Sarah Bullock is the assistant manager at the Wesley College Bookstore, a Barnes & Noble College store. She is currently a graduate student in the Master of Arts in Teaching program at Wesley College in Dover, Delaware. She lives in Delaware with her husband Kyle and their son. In the following excerpt, she recalls her memories from her grandmother's death.

I have many times wondered what she was like, my grandmother. She died when I was just six years old. When I share with others what I endured the day she died, many have told me I should be really screwed up. I guess in many ways depending on who you talk to, I am. I mean how do you stand outside your grandparents' home, knowing inside your heart that something horrible has happened and stand and wait where you are told? I remember thinking first that it was my grandfather Francis who died because he had been sick with what they called "cancer." As a kid, I just knew he was in a hospital bed at home. I hated him for it because his sickness meant that my mom wasn't home much. She had to do her family duty and take care of him when the nurses couldn't. But then as I stood there and heard the gunshots, I knew it wasn't my grandfather. I must have been numb because I don't remember my reaction. I just remember waiting and waiting. Then the ambulance came, and I watched as the EMTs took a stretcher into the house. I must have followed them in because I remember seeing her in her chair hunched over and Grandfather saying she wouldn't come when he called her. Then I watched them zip her up in a body bag and take her out on the stretcher. The gunshot had nothing to do with her death. My mom had been trying to call the house and got no answer and asked my uncle to come. Well, he decided that their pet German shepherd would be overly aggressive and territorial and decided to shoot the dog, dead, as he broke open the back door to get in. Now years later, I wonder why they didn't have a key.

Reaction to Writing

1. Underline all the instances where Sarah uses "I." Do you think she uses "I" too frequently or not? Why?

2. How else does Sarah reveal herself in this narration?

3. What are some of the important details that help you recreate Sarah's memory in your own mind?

4. How does Sarah arrange what happens in her story?

THE WRITING PROCESS—BRAINSTORMING

Writing is a process that involves brainstorming (often called pre-writing), drafting, revising, and editing. When managing your time for a writing project, it's important to give yourself enough time for each part of the process.

You will also find that writing is messy work. Rarely does writing follow any ordered steps despite what the word "process" implies. You will find yourself moving among the four parts of the writing process in a back and forth motion. For example, you will brainstorm, then draft, then brainstorm some more, then do some revising, and then back to drafting. This is perfectly normal. All professional writers move in this (often crazy) back and forth motion.

Generally, all writers have to start somewhere, and that is with brainstorming. "Brainstorming" is a good word in that you are literally storming your brain for ideas. You should think a lot about what it is that you are going to write. This is my favorite part of the writing process, although sometimes writers can find themselves never moving from the brainstorming step to the actual writing. You have to make a commitment to your ideas eventually.

Brainstorming can be as simple as talking with a friend about your ideas for a writing project. Think about how you solve any problem, and this is the way brainstorming works for writing too. Maybe you brainstorm when you're showering in the morning or when you're working out at the gym. You could also engage in some other creative activity such as drawing or doodling in order to discover the direction you want your writing to go.

The two important concepts to understand about brainstorming is (1) all writers need to have the time for the thinking that is involved when they are planning a writing project, and (2) all writers have to have a way of recording that thinking. Sometimes our best ideas come to us right away and sometimes they don't. You have to be willing to be flexible with each writing assignment that you are given. Also, don't be worried about coming up with ideas that don't work out in the long run. Writing is a bit like learning a musical instrument. As long as you keep at it, by practicing, you will fine tune it to work for you.

TOPIC SENTENCES

Focused writers try to start paragraphs with a topic sentence. Topic sentences are generally the first sentence of each paragraph. They forecast for the reader what to expect in the rest of the paragraph.

Consider a prompt given to Richard to write a paragraph describing a mistake he has made. Now, in order to develop his narrowed topic, Richard thinks about all of the mistakes he has made. Once he has decided on a narrowed topic that can be adequately covered in one paragraph, he then sets out to write his topic sentence.

Here is some advice when you are ready to write your topic sentence:

○ Be focused and specific. Use only your narrowed topic not the assigned topic.
    Avoid: "I have made many mistakes."
○ Consider your position. What is the main point you want to make about your narrowed topic? What is your position about your narrowed topic?
○ Think about how you are going to justify your position in the paragraph following the topic sentence.
○ Have strength. Consider using your narrowed topic as the subject of your sentence.
    Avoid what I refer to as throat-clearing: "When asked to write a paragraph about a mistake I made, I had to think awhile."

Avoid the throwaway sentence: "There are many mistakes made by many people."

Avoid using "I think": "I think a mistake I made was when…"

Avoid using "I will": "In this paragraph, I will describe a mistake I made."

For this particular paragraph, Richard decides that his narrowed topic will be the time he and his friends vandalized the front porch of a neighbor of his.

He writes the following topic sentence to begin his paragraph:

Vandalizing my neighbor's front porch during my junior year in high school was a costly and embarrassing mistake.

Topic sentences have four main components:

They are focused and make a specific point.

They provide a position about your specific point.

They can be justified (explained or proven) in the remaining paragraph.

They are strong.

Prompt 3.2 – Narration Prompts

Write a narrative paragraph that uses the skills discussed in this chapter. Choose from the following list:

Write about a mistake you made.

Write about a time when you were misunderstood by a family member.

Write about an achievement that made you proud of yourself.

Write about a time when you taught something to someone younger than you.

Write about a time when you did something silly.

Brainstorming Your Topic

After selecting one of the prompts in Prompt 3.2, you need to decide on your narrowed topic. Or perhaps when you selected the prompt, an idea came to you immediately for your narrowed topic. Here are some ways to generate enough details for your narrative paragraph:

1. List all the memories that you can think of in regards to your narrowed topic.

2. Choose something from the list and free-write for ten minutes. Describe as much as possible. List all the details from all your senses (sight, sound, taste, smell, and touch) for your chosen moment.

3. Reread your free-write and mark something that surprises you—a place where you wrote something unexpected.

4. List questions in regards to what you've written, questions you still have, and questions others will have.

When you have completed this brainstorming, talking about what you have generated is a perfect next step.

FRAGMENTS

Fragments appear to look like sentences by having a capital letter to begin them and punctuation such as a period to end them. However, fragments are created by the following grammatical errors:

1. They are missing a subject or a predicate or both. When a structure is missing both a subject and a predicate, it is a phrase.

2. They are dependent clauses and not independent clauses.

*** Do you remember from Chapter 2 that sentences are the same as independent clauses?

Fragments are used all the time in our speaking. They are also used by professional writers as a special technique, but generally you should avoid fragments in academic writing.

Fragment missing a predicate:

 <u>Brian having no money with him</u>.

Fragment missing a subject:

 <u>Needed to find an ATM</u>.

Fragment missing both a subject and a predicate (a prepositional phrase):

 <u>In the next hour</u>.

A complete sentence is formed when all three examples from above are combined.

 Brian, having no money with him, needed to find an ATM in the next hour.

Fragment that is a dependent clause:

 <u>Because she was late getting home from work</u>. Mary Ann had to order dinner.

Dependent words are words that can create a dependent clause (also called subordinating conjunctions).

TABLE 3.2 Words That Can Create Dependent Clauses		
after	if only	unless
although	in order that	until
as	once	what (whatever)
because	now that	when (whenever)
before	provided that	where (wherever)
even if	since	whereas
even though	so that	whether
how	than	which (whichever)
if	though	while

You certainly do not need to memorize this list of dependent words. An easy test is to first take a sentence that you know is a complete sentence, like the one from Chapter 2:

> It snowed. (complete sentence)

Now add a word to it in order to test if this word creates a dependent clause.

> Because it snowed. (fragment)
> However it snowed. (complete sentence)

Note that *however* is a transitional word and not a word that can create a dependent clause. When determining whether a structure is indeed a sentence, you should also realize that the length of a structure has little to do with whether it is a complete sentence or a fragment.

Because

You might have learned in the past that you cannot begin a sentence with "because." This is simply not true. Perhaps this advice was offered to you because your teachers wanted you to avoid creating a fragment. If you start a sentence with "because," then you will create a dependent clause that needs to be followed by an independent clause, as in the following example:

> Because it snowed, classes were cancelled for the remainder of the week.

Notice that when a dependent clause is followed by an independent clause, a comma separates them.

> Dependent clause **,** Independent clause **.**

When a dependent clause follows an independent clause, a comma is not needed unless a contrast is being made, or the dependent clause is an afterthought.

> Classes were cancelled for the remainder of the week because it snowed.
> Classes were cancelled for the remainder of the week, although they will have to be made up online. (A contrast is being made with *although*.)

There are other words to watch out for when it comes to creating fragments. These words often introduce examples or provide explanations.

> *just*   *only*   *such as*   *especially*   *for example*   *for instance*   *also*   *like*   *mainly*

> Many countries are now importing American automobiles. <u>For example, Great Britain.</u>
> General Motors has seen an increase in its exports. <u>Such as its mid-sized trucks.</u>
> I thought of other ways to get out of my locked apartment. <u>For example, through the window.</u> I hate climbing out of windows. <u>Especially from the third floor.</u>
> I thought of other ways to get out of my locked apartment, for example through the window. I hate climbing out of windows, especially from the third floor. (complete sentences)

Other words to watch out for because they can cause fragments are the relative pronouns: *that, which, who, whom,* and *whose.*

> That is exactly my point. (complete sentence)
>
> That it snowed. (fragment)
>
> Who is my roommate? (complete sentence)
>
> Who is my roommate. (fragment)

When using *who* and *that,* it is important that you remember that *who* is used with people and *that* is used for everything else.

> NO: You never know the people *that* will turn on you.
>
> YES: You never know the people *who* will turn on you.

When determining whether a sentence is indeed a complete sentence, it's important to consider the structure rather than the meaning.

Determine whether the following structure is a fragment or a complete sentence:

> For it remained to be seen by him differently.

You are probably asking yourself, "What is *it*? Who is he? *Differently* than what?" You also might recognize that *for* is one of the FANBOYS (for, and, nor, but, or, yet, so) known as a conjunction. The above structure is indeed a complete sentence. It's easier to see this in context with sentences prior to it.

Theresa's relationship with Tom was so dramatic. Even the way he broke up with her was pure drama. Tom blamed Theresa for everything wrong in his life. For it remained to be seen by him differently.

Two important concepts come from this example:

1. When determining whether a structure is a complete sentence or a fragment, consider the structure rather than meaning.

2. Complete sentences can start with one of the FANBOYS, despite what you might have been told in the past.

Yet another cause of fragments is the *–ing* verb functioning as a modifier.

> I was driving as fast as I could. <u>Hoping to get there on time</u>. (fragment)
>
> Hoping to get there on time, I was driving as fast as I could. (complete sentence)
>
> I was driving as fast as I could, hoping to get there on time. (complete sentence)

Finally, fragments can be caused by the structure of *to* and a verb functioning as a modifier.

> Each week the news broadcasts a consumer watch. <u>To tell viewers about potential scams</u>.
>
> Each week the news broadcasts a consumer watch to tell viewers about potential scams. (complete sentence)

BOX 3.1

> **Five Ways Fragments Occur**
>
> 1. They are missing a subject, a predicate, or both.
> 2. They are dependent clauses.
> 3. They are examples or explanations.
> 4. They are misusing the *–ing* verbs.
> 5. They are misusing the structure of *to* and a verb.

EXERCISE 3.1—Finding Fragments

In this nonsensical passage, determine which structures are complete sentences and which are fragments. Remember to consider structure and not meaning. Circle the number for all fragments.

(1) An ardito cabeeded with a monsha. (2) The monsha cabeeding the ardito. (3) When the ardito cabeeded the monsha. (4) That the monsha cabeeded. (5) The monsha was cabeeded by the ardito. (6) Within the monsha's cabeeding. (7) Therefore, it cabeeded the monsha. (8) Although the monsha was cabeeded. (9) And the ardito was cabeeded. (10) The monsha, however, was cabeeded. (11) Whenever the monsha cabeeds. (12) The ardito is cabeeded thoroughly. (14) At the cabeeding. (15) The cabeeding of the ardito by the monsha.

EXERCISE 3.2—Finding Fragments

In the following paragraphs, determine which structures are complete sentences and which are fragments. Circle the number for all fragments. Be prepared to explain why a fragment is indeed a fragment (see Box 3.1).

(1) By now, everyone knows the dangers of texting while driving. (2) Many states have created laws. (3) To convince drivers how dangerous the practice is. (4) Although the public might not know about the liability a text sender might incur. (5) Sending a text to someone who the sender knows is driving can be a crime. (6) If the driver causes an accident looking at the sender's text.

(7) In September of 2009, David Kubert and his wife, Linda, were motorcycling in Morris County, New Jersey. (8) Kyle Best, an eighteen-year-old, texting while driving. (9) Crossed the centerline and hit the Kuberts on their Harley. (10) Both the Kuberts had legs amputated. (11) As a result of Kyle texting while driving. (12) The Kuberts sued Kyle for negligent driving. (13) And settled for $500,000.

(14) Later the Kuberts sued Kyle's girlfriend, Shannon Colonna. (15) Who was texting Kyle when he crossed the centerline, hitting the Kuberts. (16) At the trial, the judge dismissed the case. (17) But the Kuberts appealed. (18) Contending Shannon shares responsibility with Kyle. (19) The appeals court upheld the earlier court's decision. (20) And dismissed the case. (21) However, the appeals court gave a different opinion about the case. (22) Stating that the sender of a text can possibly be liable. (23) If an accident happens as a result of the sender texting a driver. (24) Who the sender knows is driving.

CHAPTER 4
Details

© 2014 mironov. Used under license from Shutterstock, Inc.

© 2014 Alena Ozerova. Used under license from Shutterstock, Inc.

© 2014 Tomatito. Used under license from Shutterstock, Inc.

© 2014 Eugene Sergeev. Used under license from Shutterstock, Inc.

DESCRIPTION—SHOWING, NOT TELLING

We use description all the time in our everyday lives. You are asked by a friend to describe the movie you just watched. Or you want to describe the weather at school to your mother who lives 300 miles away. Or you are asked to describe a memory in an essay for your psychology class.

Writing description consists of creating a vivid image for your reader. Remember "Show and Tell" from kindergarten? This is the practice when you brought some object to class, and you had to show it to the class and tell the class something about it. In a way, describing is a lot like the showing part of "Show and Tell." However, your reader can not see whatever it is you are trying to show. The difference between showing and telling can be seen from the following example.

I had a friend who found herself miserable in her marriage. Instead of telling me she could not stay in her marriage, she said the following: "I was doing the laundry, and I found myself unable to fold his boxer shorts like I have always done. I rolled them in a ball and threw them across the room. That's when I started packing my bags to leave."

She didn't have to say these details to me; some people might even consider them trivial. However, what she did was she *showed* me how miserable she was by describing this moment.

As a writer, you can think about description in the same way as photography. A photographer captures an image for all to see. A writer has only words to use to create a "picture" in the reader's mind.

Prompt 4.1

Consider the photos at the beginning of this chapter. Choose one to describe to another student who is unable to see the photo. Use plenty of details in your descriptive paragraph.

DEVELOPING DETAILS AND TOPIC SENTENCES

Consider that you have a choice of topics. For this particular writing assignment, you are given a prompt to write a paragraph describing a pet peeve that you have. This is the general topic; you must now choose something specific among all of the pet peeves in the world. And you might have many!

Your broad topic—A pet peeve you have

You think about all the pet peeves that you have, and after a few minutes of brainstorming, you settle on one.

Your narrowed topic—Space Invaders (those people who get just too close in public spaces)

Now, consider the following questions:

Why did you choose this narrowed topic?

I'm really bothered by people invading my personal space.

Consider Making S.E.N.S.E. (Senses, Examples, Names/Numbers, Specifics, Evidence) in order to develop some details. List these.

Senses: Remember the senses?

TO SEE: What does something LOOK like?
TO HEAR: What does something SOUND like?
TO TOUCH: What does something FEEL like?
TO SMELL: What does something SMELL like?
TO TASTE: What does something TASTE like?

After thinking about this for awhile, you list the following:

body odor, bad breath, barely clothed bodies

Examples for your narrowed topic: other students, at the pool
Names/Numbers connected to your narrowed topic: don't know if I have any
Specific information about your narrowed topic: In the elevator, at the pool, just talking too close to me
Evidence to help justify your position: people who are only a few inches away from me / they make my skin crawl

You generally will not be able to cover all five of the detail-developing prompts of SENSE. That's OK. This is an exercise to fully develop your thinking about your topic.

Now, think about your topic sentence.

○ Avoid throat-clearing: "When asked to write a paragraph about my pet peeve, I had to think awhile."
○ Avoid using "I think": "I think a pet peeve that bothers me most is when people invade my space."
○ Avoid using "I will": "In this paragraph, I will describe my pet peeve."
○ Consider: What is the main point you want to make about your narrowed topic? What is your position about your narrowed topic?

○ Be focused and specific. Use only your narrowed topic not the assigned topic.

○ Avoid: "I have many pet peeves."

○ Have strength. Use your narrowed topic as the subject of your sentence.

Try: The invasion of my personal space bothers me at school as well as at the pool.

By working through SENSE, you have already found material to justify and support your topic sentence.

Prompt 4.2—Description Prompts

Write a descriptive paragraph that uses the skills discussed in this chapter. Choose from the following list:

Write about a pet peeve you have.

Write about a time when you felt stress.

Write about a physical injury that you endured.

Write about your favorite restaurant.

Write about a trip that changed you in some way.

What's the Point?

When you write for an audience, which is basically anything you write outside of a personal journal, you must consider why the reader should care to read your writing. This perhaps is a bit harsh when you are thinking the reader is your teacher. However, I encourage you to consider other readers for what you write. Yes, your professor is ultimately your reader, but beyond college, you will have many readers of your writing.

Consideration of your reader is a primary goal of all writers. When you write with an audience in mind, your purpose for writing becomes clearer. As you draft a piece of writing, try to have someone in mind who will ultimately read your writing to try to understand your intended message.

It might help to think that your readers are always asking themselves, "What's the point?" when they are reading your writing. All readers read for a reason. And you might think, "My teacher has to read my writing. It's her job." This is true, but readers are generally well-intentioned. They want to care about what you have to write.

DEVELOPING DETAILS WORKSHEET

The broad topic:

Your narrowed topic:

S.E.N.S.E.

1. Sensory details: What does something or someone look like, sound like, feel like, smell like, and taste like?

2. Examples for your narrowed topic:

3. Names/Numbers connected to your narrowed topic:

4. Specific information about your narrowed topic:

5. Evidence to help justify your position:

RUN-ONS AND COMMA SPLICES

I remember that when I was in college, I had a professor who always commented that I had run-on sentences in my essays. I had absolutely no idea what he was referring to! I figured that I was trying to write too much in one sentence—like a runaway train that could not be stopped. I'm not sure when I learned what a run-on really was.

A run-on sentence is basically two or more sentences that are within only one sentence. For this reason, run-ons are also called fused sentences. Similar to an electrician who fuses, or connects, wires, writers create the error of a run-on sentence when they string together two or more sentences within one sentence.

Here are some examples:

- ○ John had no idea where his cat was he had left him out by mistake.
- ○ Cheyenne is almost ready to go to the grocery store she needs a lot of items to prepare Thanksgiving dinner.
- ○ Bev made the cheerleading squad her senior year finally she has been trying out for four years.

It should be clear where periods belong in these sentences.

- ○ John had no idea where his cat was. He had left him out by mistake.
- ○ Cheyenne is almost ready to go to the grocery store. She needs a lot of items to prepare Thanksgiving dinner.
- ○ Bev made the cheerleading squad her senior year finally. She has been trying out for four years.

Incidentally, a lot of grammar check programs do not signal run-on sentences. This is another case when you have to be smarter than your computer.

Comma Splices

A kind of run-on sentence is known as a comma splice. Splicing is the act of putting two things together. Film-makers splice film when they edit scenes out and have to connect the film. When writers use a comma to splice, or connect, two complete sentences, they have committed an error known as a comma splice.

Here are some examples:

- ○ The maple tree had to be cut down, it stood right where the new parking garage was going to be built.
- ○ Before a big game, Jeremy, who is a linebacker, eats a lot of pasta and bread, he says it gives him energy.

The comma splices occur where actually a period should be.

- ○ The maple tree had to be cut down. It stood right where the new parking garage was going to be built.
- ○ Before a big game, Jeremy, who is a linebacker, eats a lot of pasta and bread. He says it gives him energy.

Again, grammar check software rarely finds comma splices, a form of a run-on sentence. You must be able to catch these errors yourself.

Comma splices cause confusion for readers. When readers see a comma, they believe that something other than another complete sentence will follow it.

Fixing Run-ons and Comma Splices

The easiest fix for a run-on sentence is to insert a period to separate the complete sentences that were fused together. And for a comma splice, a writer just has to turn the comma into a period. In order to create sentence variety, there are three other methods to correct run-ons and comma splices.

Consider the following example of a comma splice:

> Ben knew that he could make it through the long final exam, then he would be free to enjoy the holidays with his family.

The above example has a comma splice after *exam*.

*** Be careful with the word *then*. It often occurs in run-ons and comma splices.

The first way to correct the comma splice is to change the comma into a period.

> Ben knew that he could make it through the long final exam. Then he would be free to enjoy the holidays with his family.

The second way a run-on or comma splice can be fixed is with a semicolon. Semicolons are good separators between sentences if the sentences are similar in terms of content and structure.

> Ben knew that he could make it through the long final exam; then he would be free to enjoy the holidays with his family.

Notice that after semicolons, there is no capitalization. The formula for using a semicolon is as follows:

> Complete sentence**;** complete sentence**.**

A third way to correct the error is by using the comma and inserting one of the FANBOYS (for, and, nor, but, or, yet, so). Two complete sentences or independent clauses can be connected with a comma and one of these conjunctions. This is called a compound sentence. Take note that the comma goes **before** the conjunction.

> Ben knew that he could make it through the long final exam, so then he would be free to enjoy the holidays with his family.

It is important to choose one of the FANBOYS that make sense in terms of meaning. Each one has a slightly different meaning.

BOX 4.1

FANBOYS and Their Meanings

For – because
And – in addition
Nor – neither choice
But – a contrast
Or – a choice
Yet – at this time or a contrast
So – as a result

The fourth way to fix a run-on or a comma splice is to change one of the independent clauses to a dependent clause. You might remember this from the discussion of fragments in Chapter 3. Dependent words create dependent clauses which are fragments when they stand on their own. Table 3.2 lists some of these dependent words. Let's return to our example:

> Ben knew that he could make it through the long final exam, then he would be free to enjoy the holidays with his family.

We could turn the first independent clause into a dependent clause with the word *if*. *If* and *then* often work together.

> If Ben knew that he could make it through the long final exam, then he would be free to enjoy the holidays with his family.

Notice this changes the meaning of the sentence. This is one of the reasons writers use dependent clauses.

*** Remember that when a dependent clause is followed by an independent clause, a comma separates them.

> Dependent clause **,** independent clause **.**

We could also change the second independent clause into a dependent clause with the word *because*.

> Ben knew that he could make it through the long final exam because then he would be free to enjoy the holidays with his family.

*** Remember when a dependent clause follows an independent clause, a comma is not needed unless a contrast is being made.

BOX 4.2

Four Methods to Fix Run-ons and Comma Splices

(A): Fix comma splice or run-on by making two sentences, using a period.

(B): Fix comma splice or run-on by using a semicolon.

(C): Fix comma splice or run-on by using a comma and one of the FANBOYS.

(D): Fix comma splice or run-on by using a dependent word (subordinator).

EXERCISE 4.1—Finding Comma Splices and Fragments

Circle a comma that functions as a comma splice and put "CS" above it. Underline a fragment and put "FRAG" beside it.

Often there is the problem of a sentence that is not a sentence. Like in advertising. But in academic writing, we need to be careful of writing sentences that are not complete because our readers are savvy and educated, we need to be concerned about paying attention to our sentences. Sometimes a sentence will read like one sentence, but it needs to be two. In some cases sentences are understandable, that does not justify sloppiness or making your readers work harder. Readers who might be grading you or paying you. Sentences become more complex as your ideas become more complex, therefore your knowledge of mechanics and punctuation needs to grow as well. When I decided to learn how to make complex sentences, my writing really improved.

Many college students do not have an understanding of grammar from their prior education, they are not at a disadvantage if they're willing to work hard at it now. Also sometimes they don't see the point. Consideration of your reader is something that will help you, and your future employers will sit up and take notice. Many of my friends work in prestigious jobs, their number one complaint is employees who cannot write well. Good writing matters. And good thinking. When we're able to combine our complicated thinking and our sophisticated writing, we can really impress our readers. It's not just knowing grammar and what a specific term is called. For example, an antecedent. I'm a firm believer that you don't need to know the grammar terms to write well, and with precision, you will be more easily understood. No one likes to be misunderstood, and no one likes to read and reread a sentence many times to understand it. By studying up on it, your sentences will improve, your prose will gain style, and readers will marvel at your complicated ideas. Not your complicated sentences.

EXERCISE 4.2—Fixing Comma Splices and Run-ons

For the following exercise, first determine if the sentence contains a comma splice or if it is a run-on. If it is correct, write "correct" below the sentence. If you determine the sentence has a comma splice or it is a run-on, correct it by writing the revised sentence below the sentence, using the method designated at the end of the sentence (A, B, C, or D). Make sure you use correct punctuation and proofread your work.

Methods to correct a comma splice or run-on

(A): Fix comma splice or run-on by making two sentences, using a period.

(B): Fix comma splice or run-on by using a semicolon.

(C): Fix comma splice or run-on by using a comma and one of the FANBOYS.

(D): Fix comma splice or run-on by using a dependent word (subordinator):

after	if/if only	until
although	now that	what(ever)
as	once	when(ever)
because	since	where

1. March Madness refers to the time of the year when college basketball teams from across the country compete to be the National Collegiate Athletic Association (NCAA®) champion. (A)

2. Both men's and women's Division I teams compete, although not against one another, that competition would be really interesting. (B)

3. In 2014, sixty-eight men's college basketball teams represented their schools in the tournament, it's their opportunity to showcase their players at a national level. (C)

4. Some players refer to the NCAA® tournament as the "Big Dance," with players saying they are going to the Big Dance. (D)

5. Thousands of Americans try out their ability at picking the champion, dwindling the sixty-eight teams in four brackets to the big winner, this contest involves a lot of luck and is often called "Bracketology." (A)

6. In 2014, Warren Buffett, an investment guru, offered one billion dollars to anyone who could correctly pick all the winning teams in the match-ups, a feat that is virtually impossible. (B)

7. By the time the "Sweet Sixteen" had won, this title refers to the remaining sixteen teams after three rounds of games, no one was left with a correct bracket. (C)

8. In fact, of the sixteen teams remaining, three teams had rankings in the double-digits the rankings are one through sixteen in the four brackets. (D)

9. March Madness is always fun with thousands of fans cheering on their teams and their brackets the excitement comes generally at the same time as the arrival of spring. (A)

10. It is a time for Americans to have some fun after a long cold winter, this was especially true of the winter of 2014, which many Americans found especially cold and snowy. (B)

11. By the time the Final Four had won, only one team that was ranked as number one was left, the University of Florida managed to get to the Final Four. (C)

12. For only the second time in tournament history, two teams with rankings of seven and eight remained in the Final Four University of Connecticut and Kentucky moved on for the 2014 challenge. (D)

ILLUSTRATION – SHOWING EXAMPLES

Similarly to how description shows details, illustration shows examples. For this reason, illustration is also called exemplification. Think about how descriptions create vivid images for a reader. In the same way, illustrations provide representations of an idea for a reader. For illustration, you develop examples from a specific topic. How many examples you show is determined from the length of your assignment. The key is that you want to show the best examples for the size of your writing project, and you want to have enough to get your point across.

Illustration—A Student's Paragraph

George, a freshman in a Basic Writing course, wrote the following illustration paragraph. His assignment is as follows:

> Your second formal assignment is a paragraph illustrating a trend you have observed among people in your peer group. The trend might involve something physical—such as clothing or a type of hairstyle— or it might involve an attitude, a belief, or a common problem. In developing your paragraph, be sure to provide specific examples from your experience and observations.

Copying the Look

> Have you ever noticed how much musicians influence the hairstyles of today's generation of young adults? I have certainly noticed this trend with my friends and myself. My friend Barry loves rap music, and his favorite rapper is Wiz Khalifa. Wiz has a blonde patch in the front of his hair. Barry could not wait to get the same blonde patch bleached into the front of his head. Everyone knew that Barry was copying Wiz Khalifa's look. Another friend of mine from high school is Verna. Verna loves the R&B singer Rihanna. One day during our senior year, Verna came to school with long hair on the right side of her head and a shaved head on her left. When I asked her how she got this crazy idea, she said that she saw Rihanna's new music video. The only difference was Rihanna's left side is long and her right side is shaved. I even copied the look of another rapper, Waka Flocka. He is light-skinned and tall like me. Because he has dreadlocks, I decided to grow them, so I would look even more like him. Musicians not only draw us to their music, but also to their look.

Notice how George used three specific examples to make the point that he and his peers copy the hairstyles of popular musicians. This amount seemed to be enough examples for one paragraph to make his point about the trend of copying the look of musicians.

Prompt 4.3—Illustration Prompts

Write an illustrative paragraph that uses details and has specific examples for your narrowed topic. Choose from the following list of broad topics:

A trend among your peers

Celebrity bad behavior

Dangers of driving

Problems with today's high schools

Commercialization of holidays

THE WRITING PROCESS—DRAFTING

"How do I know what I think until I see what I say?"

E.M. Forster

Remember to give yourself plenty of time for all of the parts of the writing process: brainstorming, drafting, revising, and editing. After the planning and brainstorming have provided enough material to get started, it is time to begin writing your project, otherwise known as drafting. Drafting is creating your first draft. In fact, writing could be seen as never being finished. Even if you hand in a final draft to a professor for a grade, it is still a final *draft*. You could return to this piece of writing years later to revise it. That can be a frustrating part of writing. It is never truly finished, but you do have to feel like you have finished at some point.

You might be asking yourself, "How do I finally stop procrastinating and start drafting?" Consider the following tips to getting started on the actual writing.

Decide whether you will be putting pen to paper or drafting right on to the computer. Some writing projects might seem easier to handwrite first, and others you can draft using your keyboard. And drafting for some writing projects could be a combination of handwriting and typing.

Get comfortable with your surroundings. Much research has shown that writing requires concentration and distractions will not be your friend. Most writers draft by themselves in fairly quiet environments. Your best writing will not happen in a room full of distractions.

Draft quickly and don't stop. You should make drafting easy for yourself. If you get stuck on finding the right word or remembering some detail, then you have caused yourself to be distracted. Use some sort of marking system in your draft to signal to yourself that this area needs attention for whatever reason.

Use all of your details, examples, and evidence that support your main points. Remember that you have given yourself time to revise and possibly eliminate support that does not seem to work for this writing project.

When you are finished with a specific period of time for your drafting, by all means, back up your work! Computers are notorious for causing chaos in all writers' lives. In addition to backing up your work in some way other than a hard drive that can suddenly crash for some unknown reason, you can also back up your work by printing a hard copy.

Reward yourself at the end of a drafting session. You now can say you were writing your project and not just thinking about writing it.

ADJECTIVES AND ADVERBS

Adjectives

Adjectives describe nouns and pronouns. These often answer the questions "What kind?" (*big*) "How many?" (*five*) and Which one(s)? (*those*).

Those five big dogs all belong to my sister.

Adjectives are especially helpful for describing and illustrating because of the details needed for these two purposes. Many adjectives end with *–ful*, *-ish*, *-less* and *–like*. As an example, consider the word *child*. How different is it be *childish* than it is to be *childlike*? How about to be *childless*? That is entirely different.

Adjectives are important to our language, and adding many to your vocabulary is a good goal to have. Fortunately, adjectives are quite plentiful in the English language. Here are just a few common adjectives:

angry	funny	old	salty	sweet
big	green	one	scary	tall
black	happy	orange	seven	ten
blue	hard	pink	short	thick
brown	large	poor	six	thin
dry	little	pretty	sleepy	three
eight	long	purple	slow	two
fast	loud	quiet	small	weak
fat	mean	red	smooth	wet
five	new	rich	soft	white
four	nice	rough	sour	yellow
friendly	nine	sad	strong	young

EXERCISE 4.3—Finding Adjectives

Look back to George's illustration paragraph "Copying the Look." Circle or highlight all of the adjectives you find.

Adverbs

Adverbs describe or modify verbs, adjectives, or other adverbs. These words often end in *–ly*, like *badly*, but this is not always the case. For instance, *lovely* is an adjective.

A *lovely* woman walked into the elevator.

Adverbs answer the questions "How?" "How much?" "Where?" "When?" "Why?" and "To what extent?"

He <u>carefully</u> carried the baby. (answers "How?")
He could hold the baby <u>forever</u>. (answers "To what extent?")

Here are just a few common adverbs:

almost	deeply	kindly	proudly
always	eagerly	lightly	quickly
angrily	early	loudly	quietly
anxiously	easily	lowly	rarely
awfully	energetically	naturally	safely
boldly	excitedly	nearly	secretly

bravely	finally	neatly	silently
briefly	fully	nervously	sleepily
brightly	gently	never	slowly
carefully	greatly	oddly	softly
cheerfully	happily	patiently	sweetly
correctly	heavily	playfully	usually

An adjective often is found in front of the noun or pronoun it describes; however, an adverb can be found before or after the verb, adjective, or other adverb it modifies. When determining whether to use an adjective or an adverb, you have to know what part of speech it is modifying.

Good, Well, Bad, and Badly

In this chapter, you used the senses (look, smell, sound, taste, and feel) to develop details. These same senses when used as verbs often work in a function referred to as linking verbs.

He looked tired.

She felt happy.

The laundry smelled fresh.

Linking verbs also include forms of the *be* verb (*am, was, is, are*) and other verbs that have a sense of being or becoming (*seem, grow, turn, stay, remain*). Linking verbs connect nouns and pronouns to adjectives. *Tired, happy,* and *fresh* in the prior examples are all adjectives. When determining whether to use an adjective or an adverb, it is important to determine whether the verb in the sentence is functioning as a linking verb or just a verb.

He <u>looked</u> deep in thought. (*looked* is a linking verb / *deep* is an adjective)

He <u>looked</u> deeply into her eyes. (*looked* is a verb / *deeply* is an adverb)

Complications arise with the words *good, well, bad,* and *badly.* The word *good* is always used as an adjective. When the word *well* is referring to health, it is an adjective. Other than this health reference, *well* is an adverb.

NO:	Alex did good in calculus.
YES:	Alex did well in calculus.
YES:	I feel well enough to go to class today. (*Well* is referring to health.)
MAYBE:	Jeremy smells well. (If the intended meaning here is that Jeremy has a good sense of smell, then *well* is an adverb, and this is correct.)
YES:	Jeremy smells good with his new cologne.

When answering the question, "How are you feeling?" you can answer correctly, "I feel good" or "I feel well."

The word *bad* is always used as an adjective, and the word *badly* is always used as an adverb.

NO:	I felt badly this morning. (This means my sense of touch, or feeling with my fingers, was not good this morning.)
YES:	I felt bad this morning.

Every day, and *Everyday*

Every day as two words is the adjective *every* followed by the noun *day*. *Everyday* as one word is an adjective that means on a daily basis.

It was becoming difficult for Marjorie to get out of bed every day. Her depression has become an everyday feeling.

EXERCISE 4.4—Choosing Adjectives or Adverbs

Circle the correct adjective or adverb for each sentence. Underline the word that the adjective or adverb is modifying.

1. Some restaurants are focused (sole / solely) on chicken like Buffalo Wild Wings® and Kentucky Fried Chicken®.

2. Chicken ranks number one (over / overly) beef, pork, and fish for American families' home-cooked meals.

3. (Literal / Literally) hundreds of recipes can be made that taste (good / well).

4. Chicken can be made into (delicious / deliciously) pasta and stew recipes.

5. My favorite is fried chicken, although it is (probable / probably) a (bad / badly) choice because of the frying.

6. I (previous / previously) knew a boy who would eat only chicken nuggets (every day / everyday).

7. Even my sister who is a (bad / badly) cook can make chicken noodle soup that (actual / actually) tastes (good / well).

8. Now people are choosing (organic / organically) raised chickens, or some people are raising chickens in their own backyards.

9. This (easy / easily) white meat can be made to please all tastes and (cultural / culturally) traditions.

10. Mexicans and Asians (proud / proudly) use chicken in an (abundant / abundantly) amount of their recipes like burritos and kung pao chicken (respective / respectively).

CHAPTER 5

Connection

Photo courtesy of James G. and Elizabeth R. Troutman.

UNITY

A piece of writing has unity when all of it is focused on the main point. When readers sense that an idea is out of place or is unconnected to the main point, unity might be lacking. Unity means all the ideas stand together and are focused on the main idea.

The topic sentence helps maintain unity in a paragraph. The topic sentence makes a promise to the reader as to what to expect in the remaining paragraph, but it also helps the writer draft a paragraph. By always having your topic sentence as a guide, you can achieve unity in your paragraphs.

EXERCISE 5.1—Unity

Read the following paragraph and underline the topic sentence. Then find the area in the paragraph where the writer loses unity and place an * next to it.

Lowering the drinking age from twenty-one to eighteen years of age will have too many bad consequences. Young people like to binge drink, and it seems that now the goal for teens is to see who can black out first. Teens are affected too much by peer pressure. I have been to many parties where everyone is trying to outdo everyone else in how much they can drink. Eighteen-year-olds just don't know how to make good decisions. Another bad consequence for lowering the drinking age is drunk driving. Teens have very limited experience behind the wheel of a car. If they were allowed to drink legally and then drive, there would be so many more tragic accidents. Finally, teens' brains have not fully developed, and consumption of alcohol on a regular basis could have bad effects for the brain's development. With peer pressure, drunk driving, and young brains still developing, lowering the drinking age to eighteen is a bad idea.

Writing a Concluding Sentence

How you end your paragraph can help the unity of it as well. A good concluding sentence gives the reader a sense that your paragraph is wrapped up tightly. You have the opportunity with your last sentence to add an opinion based on the support that you have provided.

- A concluding sentence draws attention to what you have written.
- A concluding sentence references the main point of your paragraph.
- A concluding sentence should never repeat your topic sentence. That sentence is already in your paragraph at the beginning.
- A concluding sentence should not introduce new or unrelated ideas in order to keep the unity of your paragraph.

○ A concluding sentence is used to avoid stopping abruptly in a way that it seems like the paragraph is unfinished, that you simply reached your length requirement, or that you ran out of time.

○ A concluding sentence should not change your focus or position.

COHERENCE

A piece of writing has coherence when all the sentences are connected in terms of the words used and in terms of the sentence structure. Student writers like to judge a piece of writing that has coherence by saying, "It has flow." This means it is easy for the reader to move from one sentence to the next. The sentences seem to want to be placed next to one another.

Transitional expressions are an excellent tool to coherence. With transitions between words and sentences, a reader is more easily able to move along in the reading of a paragraph. Box 5.1 lists some common transitional expressions and the relationships they signal.

BOX 5.1

Transitional Expressions and Their Relationships

Addition: also, too, in addition, and, furthermore, additionally, as well as, likewise, similarly, in the same way

Contrast: although, but, however, instead, on the other hand, yet, conversely

Example: for example, for instance, namely, specifically, thus

Causes or Results: because, as a result, therefore, so, consequently, finally

Summary: in brief, in summary, hence, in conclusion, finally

Time: first, second, third, next, then, soon, finally, before, afterward, meanwhile, eventually, currently, during, after, last, since, when, while

Place: here, there, nearby, above, across, beyond, next to, opposite, to the left, to the right, in the front, in the back, in the distance, under, where

Importance: in fact, especially, in particular, more important, most important, above all

---

Another way to make sure your writing has coherence is repetition. Repeating key words and phrases can help your reader understand your overall focus more and gives your reader a sense that your writing flows well and has a connection.

A third way to achieve coherence is through the use of pronouns. Instead of repeating the same nouns over and over again, pronouns can substitute for these nouns, creating a sense of coherence for the reader to follow easily.

Notice how repetition of key words (bolded) and pronouns (underlined) work to promote coherence in the following paragraph.

People continue to think they can get **colds** from circumstances other than a **virus**. When the weather changes dramatically, I always hear **people** say that now everyone is going to get sick. They also warn against going outside in the **cold** without wearing a jacket or with wet hair. In their minds, cold **temperatures** cause **colds**, but **people** get **colds** in the **summer** time too. And we witness dramatic **temperature** changes in the **summer** as well. The only way to **avoid** getting a **cold** is to **avoid** getting the **virus**. Washing our hands and **avoiding** the airborne travelling germs of the **cold virus** are the best way to **avoid** getting a **cold**.

EXERCISE 5.2—Transitions

Fill in the missing transitions in the paragraphs below. Use Box 5.1 to make sure the transition you select indicates the accurate relationship. Try to use as many different transitions as possible.

Many studies have shown that changing our everyday routines and occurrences leads to maintaining the health of our minds. _____ , changing the ringtones on your cell phone might benefit your brain. It is good for the brain to encounter new things _____ , even if it is as simple as the sound of someone calling you. _____, I have a friend Ruth who changes her ringtones once a month. _____, she has a different ringtone for each of her close friends and family members.

When we get out of our routines, we keep our brains healthy and active. _____, changing which hand you use to brush your teeth can provide brain benefits. _____, the same is true for changing which hand you use to operate your computer mouse. Engaging in new activities can help our minds to work optimally _____. If you like working with numbers, then you can try doing crossword puzzles. _____ if you are more of a language person, you can try Sudoku. _____, if you never tried playing a musical instrument, then take a few lessons. _____, changing your drive to work or school is another way to stay out of a rut. The brain needs to be constantly challenged by new and different routines.

EXERCISE 5.3—Repetition

Highlight or underline the areas where coherence is achieved with repetition.

Millions of Americans have gotten caught up in the zombie craze. With television shows like *The Walking Dead* and movies like *Zombieland*, Americans can indulge their fascination with zombies. Zombies were regular human beings until they are bitten by a human-flesh-craving zombie. Then a person becomes a zombie, craving human flesh too.

Zombies possess no intelligence, and they are quite slow. They look like dead people who have crawled out of their graves to prey on people. Zombies cannot talk and cannot communicate. Regular human beings have to avoid zombies for the obvious reason that they do not want to become the walking dead.

Americans' fascination with zombies is probably connected to the drama and survival story that underlies the flesh-eating attacks. People now participate in zombie races and zombie contests. For Halloween, a zombie was a popular costume. No one knows how long the zombie craze will last, probably a long time as survival themes persist.

ANALYSIS—EXAMINING

You will be asked to analyze continually in college and in your professional life. When we analyze, we become scientists and examine something closely as if under a microscope. An analysis seeks to find the true significance of something by examining the features of its foundation. A good analysis follows a specific guiding rule to follow when investigating these features.

For example, consider that you are asked to analyze a piece of literature, a classic novel. You could analyze this novel for numerous features: setting, characters, plot, historical context, themes, and narration. You are limited by what features you select based from your guiding rule and the length of your analysis.

A student wrote the following paragraph analyzing body piercing. Notice how she seems to create her purpose by asking why all her friends want to be pierced. She looks closely at the different kinds of piercings in order to attempt to answer her question.

Analysis—A Student's Paragraph

All of my friends, men and women, are getting body piercings, and I don't quite understand it. When I was thirteen years old, I could not wait to get my ears pierced. Five years later, I still remember the pain and the tears that sprung to my eyes at the little kiosk in the mall. My friend Ashley has her ears pierced five times on each ear. The top piercing goes through her cartilage. I asked her why she has so many piercings and she actually said that she likes the pain of the piercings. Another friend Suze wears gauges in her ears that are about the size of dimes. I asked her whether she was worried that these huge holes would never close, and she said that there is plastic surgery to fix the holes. I didn't ask her how she intends to pay for this surgery. A guy friend of mine Lee has the middle part of his nose, his septum, pierced. He said that it really hurt, but it's worth it because girls find it sexy. I have seen piercings in noses, tongues, lips, cheeks, and eyebrows. And that is just the facial region. Belly button piercings are popular among my girlfriends. They report that the belly button doesn't really hurt as much, and they love the chance to show off their belly button rings with their short tanks and bikinis. Overall, piercings seems to be about self-expression and sex appeal. I still wonder how my friends intend to land professional careers with all these holes in them.

Prompt 5.1

Write an analysis paragraph for one of the following broad topics. You will need to discover a guiding rule for your analysis to uncover the important features that you address.

A TV commercial that you and your peers find persuasive

The perfect pet

Your use of the Internet

The personality of your father or mother

Your attitude towards dating

THE SANDY HOOK ELEMENTARY SCHOOL SHOOTING

On December 14, 2012, the United States experienced another tragedy of school violence when Adam Lanza entered Sandy Hook Elementary School in Newtown, Connecticut, and started shooting innocent children, teachers, and staff. He fatally shot twenty children and six adults before turning the gun on himself. President Barack Obama had the following to say after the shooting.

"This afternoon, I spoke with Governor Malloy and FBI Director Mueller. I offered Gov. Malloy my condolences on behalf of the nation and made it clear he will have every single resource that he needs to investigate this heinous crime, care for the victims, counsel their families."

"We've endured too many of these tragedies in the past few years. And each time I learn the news, I react not as a president, but as anybody else would as a parent. And that was especially true today. I know there's not a parent in America who doesn't feel the same overwhelming grief that I do."

"The majority of those who died today were children—beautiful, little kids between the ages of five and ten years old. They had their entire lives ahead of them—birthdays, graduations, weddings, kids of their own. Among the fallen were also teachers, men and women who devoted their lives to helping our children fulfill their dreams."

"So our hearts are broken today for the parents and grandparents, sisters and brothers of these little children, and for the families of the adults who were lost."

"Our hearts are broken for the parents of the survivors, as well, for as blessed as they are to have their children home tonight, they know that their children's innocence has been torn away from them too early and there are no words that will ease their pain."

"As a country, we have been through this too many times. Whether it is an elementary school in Newtown, or a shopping mall in Oregon, or a temple in Wisconsin, or a movie theater in Aurora, or a street corner in Chicago, these neighborhoods are our neighborhoods and these children are our children. And we're going to have to come together and take meaningful action to prevent more tragedies like this, regardless of the politics."

"This evening, Michelle and I will do what I know every parent in America will do, which is hug our children a little tighter, and we'll tell them that we love them, and we'll remind each other how deeply we love one another. But there are families in Connecticut who cannot do that tonight, and they need all of us right now. In the hard days to come, that community needs us to be at our best as Americans, and I will do everything in my power as president to help, because while nothing can fill the space of a lost child or loved one, all of us can extend a hand to those in need, to remind them that we are there for them, that we are praying for them, that the love they felt for those they lost endures not just in their memories, but also in ours."

Reaction to Writing

1. President Obama has been considered a great speaker, especially in these times of tragedy. What words in particular stand out to you in this speech? Why are these words significant? Are there any instances of words that seem as if they are not quite the right choice?

2. Knowing what you now know about coherence, mark areas in the speech where you find the use of transitions and repetition.

Prompt 5.2

In one paragraph, analyze President Obama's attempt to comfort his audience. If you use any words from the speech, be sure to put quotation marks around them. Include your own reaction to the Sandy Hook Elementary School shooting.

Prompt 5.3

In one paragraph, analyze the effects of school violence on you.

SEMICOLONS

We looked at using the semicolon in the last chapter as a way to fix a run-on or a comma splice. There are other ways to use a semicolon, as well.

*** Remember that semicolons should be used only between complete sentences that are closely related in terms of content.

To show a relationship between two complete sentences a semicolon can be used with a transitional expression.

Tim will be graduating college this May; therefore, he needs to start his job search.

When a transitional expression is used after the semicolon, it must be followed with a comma. Also one of the FANBOYS (for, and, nor, but, or, yet, so) should not be used with the semicolon. If one of the FANBOYS is used to connect two complete sentences, use a comma after the complete sentence.

Complete sentence **,** FANBOYS Complete sentence.
Complete sentence **;** Complete sentence.
Complete sentence **;** Transition **,** Complete sentence.

Box 5.1 has a complete list of transitions that you can use with semicolons. It is important that you do not overuse semicolons and that you always make sure the sentences are complete and closely related.

EXERCISE 5.4—SEMICOLONS

Add semicolons and commas to the following sentences. If the sentence requires no punctuation, write "Correct."

1. Students all over America show their support for cancer awareness through their clothing, hairstyles, and jewelry but their schools do not always approve of their displays of support.

2. In 2013, an Oklahoma high school student was sent home from school for wearing a breast cancer awareness t-shirt with "Twin Peaks" on the front and "Save the Scenery" on the back consequently school officials decided the t-shirt was a distraction to student learning.

3. In the same school, other breast cancer awareness t-shirts have been worn with sayings like "Big or Small, Save Them All" and "Save Second Base" and these t-shirts were even sold at the school to raise money for breast cancer awareness.

4. A Michigan high school student was banned from competing in his school's track meets for his hot pink Mohawk his hairstyle was in support for his mother who is battling breast cancer.

5. In Colorado, a nine year old was suspended for shaving her head to show support for a friend who was going through chemotherapy although the school eventually changed its decision.

6. Two students in the seventh and eighth grades in the Easton Area School District in eastern Pennsylvania sued their school for not allowing them to wear "I ♥ boobies" bracelets.

7. The school district stated that the bracelets were lewd yet the courts supported the girls' constitutional right to free speech.

8. The American Civil Liberties Union (ACLU) provided lawyers for the girls meanwhile the ACLU was busy with the case because the school district appealed two courts' decisions.

9. Eventually the case was appealed to the United States Supreme Court the court upholded the lower courts' decisions in support of the girls' freedom of speech.

10. Now schools all over America are faced with difficult decisions about students' displays for various other causes for example students could promote other social issues like immigration, politics, and even education.

THE WRITING PROCESS—REVISING

To revise means "to see again." For a writer, going back and looking at what has been written is one of the most important parts of the writing process. Many students fear revising because of the implications that their writing will not hold up to some lofty standard. Or worse yet, they fear that they will lose all that has been written and will have to start over again. This simply is **not** true. Revising can only benefit your writing. Rarely do writers produce the final draft on their first attempt.

You have to have confidence to revise and the ability to criticize yourself. It also helps to have some distance in terms of time between drafting and revising. When you are planning a writing project, allow yourself a few days between drafting and returning to your draft to see it in a new light.

Be careful not to jump right into editing. Revising is focusing on larger issues—how the paragraph or essay works as a whole. Tinkering with a word here or there is not revising; it is editing. You will have time to edit after you deal with the larger issues first. After all, what is the sense in spending a half an hour figuring out the right word in your concluding sentence if you are going to eliminate that last sentence entirely?

Some goals and activities for revising include the following:

Look at organization. If your draft is one paragraph, focus on how your sentences add up to the paragraph's unity and coherence. If your draft is longer, focus on how your paragraphs work together. You want to make sure your writing has unity, meaning it does not go off topic anywhere, and you want to make sure it has coherence, by using transitional expressions, repetition, and pronouns.

Keep your writing situation in mind. Consider your purpose and audience when re-reading your draft critically.

Consider adding content. Many times writers find themselves engaging in more brainstorming in order to discover new ideas to add. Also, in the process of drafting, writers discover new ideas all of the time. These ideas might be better than your initial ones.

Consider deleting content. If something seems like it is off topic, then it is, and it probably should be cut from your draft. You might want to keep what you delete in a separate file. You never know when you might use this material, and it might make it easier for you to delete your hard work.

Consider moving sentences. Often, writers find certain sentences or paragraphs work in a different order.

Always return to your topic sentence. Everything written in a paragraph should have a connection to your topic sentence. It is perfectly acceptable to revise your topic sentence if during your drafting and revising, you discovered a different purpose or a slightly different narrowed topic.

PROCESS ANALYSIS—ASKING HOW?

A special kind of analysis is the process analysis. The purpose of this kind of writing is to examine how something is done or how something works. When analyzing how something is done, you can assume your readers will be reading your process analysis in order to do the same thing themselves. On the other hand, if you are writing a process analysis to explain how something works, then your aim is to provide all of the necessary information about the process.

A process analysis follows a chronological order similar to a narration where you are relating a story. Often a process analysis uses a combination of narration and analysis as you will see in the following article "A Strategic Education." It might be useful to refer to Table 3.1 for a list of transitions for time.

To form a topic sentence, try answering the following question:

What do my readers need to know about this process?

Your topic sentence should include a purpose that explains why the process in important and why the reader should find it interesting.

Often a process analysis goes beyond one paragraph, but you should try to be as clear as possible, using plain language. One challenge is to give your sentences variety, so your analysis will be read more smoothly without the choppiness of for example, a recipe. Always keep your reader in mind as you draft to make sure you do not leave out any important steps of the process. At the same time, you don't want to bore your readers with details they don't need.

"A Strategic Education" by Jennifer Kalita

The following article explains how a college student can go about finding a major that will lead to a promising career. Jennifer Kalita writes the column *Just Ask Jen*. This article originally appeared in *The Baltimore Sun* on April 15, 2012.

A STRATEGIC EDUCATION

by Jennifer Kalita

When I started college, I was convinced that there was but one career path for me: psycholo- 1
gist. I had all of the credentials an 18-year-old freshman thought necessary, including several
hours logged on the phone helping my fellow teens through one crisis after another and a genuine desire to help other people through challenging times.

This vision quickly dissolved upon taking Psychology 101 during my first semester. I was 2
bored to tears, and began to have visions of hurling people out of my office window who, week
after week, came to me to complain but didn't have the good sense to take my sound advice.

But what else was I going to study? I had no interest in medicine, law, accounting, or political 3
science. If my college degree was going to theoretically advance my career and ability to generate
an income, didn't it have to have something to do with a desired field?

In the absence of a career path that I could get excited about, I shifted gears and tried to focus 4
on my natural talents. I had two: I was good with people and I could write. I settled on an English
major (learning about what and how other people wrote in the past) and Communications minor
(learning about what and how I could write in the future).

One marketing communications class later, I was hooked. I went on to a fulfilling career in 5
marketing and public relations, where I was able to do what I wanted to do as a psychologist: help
people to think strategically, communicate better and achieve their goals. I just didn't realize then
that it would manifest in a business, rather than a therapeutic, content.

Many college students spend their freshman and sophomore years completing core classes, 6
and are well into their junior year without a clear path in mind. But by year three, it's important to
grab onto some kind of focus with both fists.

Step one: Identify your genuine interests, as well as your natural skills and talents. This is the 7
bridge to courses of study and ultimate day jobs that will resonate with you. Even if your interest
in pottery or your knack for organization don't at first seem like major clues to your ideal major,
you must begin at the beginning.

Conversely, identify that which doesn't fuel you. If you're more introverted, a career in public 8
relations may not be a great fit for you. If you can't sit at a desk for long periods of time without
twitching, avoid a career path that would keep you pinned indoors.

Can't seem to identify these things for yourself? Ask trusted family members and friends for 9
feedback. There may be clues lurking in what you said you wanted to be when you grew up or in the
fact that you organized a used toy sale for all the kids on your block when you were 8 years old.

Your daily habits are also very telling. If you love *CSI* and *Law & Order* reruns, perhaps a career
in forensic science or law enforcement makes sense. If you comb the local paper for adventurous
weekend activities, maybe a career in event planning is a logical fit.

Step two: Think through how these skills and talents can be integrated into a more strategic 10
approach to getting a degree that will serve you. Begin with assessing how your interests might
play out in the real world. Is music the only thing that makes sense to you? If all you can think
about is starting a band and hitting numero uno on the Billboard charts, think about what other
coursework will support your music major. A poetry class will help you better understand how to
compose good lyrics. A marketing minor will give you the skills you'll need to differentiate your
band and get noticed by the big recording labels.

Rather than majoring in foreign languages, consider putting your knack for Spanish to work 11
in international business with a Spanish minor. Think your skill set begins and ends with video
games? Take a look at computer science with a minor in graphic design.

Step three: Do your homework on the solid career paths of the future. From the postal system to library science, what careers are being all but eliminated by the Internet? From city management to manufacturing, what careers are being vacated by retiring boomers at an alarming rate?

12

Economist Barry Bluestone, dean of the School of Public Policy and Urban Affairs at Northeastern University, estimates there will be more than 5 million job vacancies, including 2.4 million in the education, health care, government and nonprofit sectors, over the next seven years. According to Bluestone's report, After the Recovery: Help Needed—The Coming Labor Shortage and How People in Encore Careers Can Help Solve It, "If the baby boom generation retires from the labor force at the same rate and age as current older workers, the baby bust generation that follows will likely be too small to fill many of the projected new jobs."

13

According to the U.S. Labor Department, 13 of the 20 fastest-growing careers are in health care, with home health aides, medical assistants and physician assistants in the top five. As global trade grows and changes, international business is also predicted to be a solid career track, particularly with a focus in finance or law.

14

Gone are the days when people moved on to college because it was simply the next step after high school. While a strategic educational approach is as easy as 1-2-3, it will also thoughtfully and perfectly position you for what the world needs.

15

Reaction to Writing

1. Kalita's title is "A Strategic Education." Why does she use the word *strategic*?

2. If you do not know the meanings of the following words, try to determine their meaning from the surrounding context in Kalita's article. Check their meanings in a dictionary and write a sentence using each word.

   manifest (5)

   therapeutic (5)

   resonate (7)

   introverted (8)

   integrated (11)

   differentiate (11)

3. Kalita's article is a process analysis as well as a narrative. Explain how this combination works.

4. Explain how Kalita uses statistics in her article.

Prompt 5.4

In one or more paragraphs, write a process analysis on one of the following topics. Assume your readers are reading your process analysis in order to do the same thing. It might be helpful to use second person point-of-view or "you." Be sure to start your paragraph with a topic sentence that shows your reader why this process is important.

How to waste time

How to make a relationship work

How to win at_____ (you fill in the blank)

How to study

How to drive your friend or roommate crazy

EDITED AMERICAN ENGLISH AND NONSTANDARD LANGUAGE

Edited American English is what you are striving to write when you are writing for college and for most areas of employment. This is the language that is used in popular magazines and newspapers like *Newsweek* and *The New York Times*. Edited American English is a language that you are quite used to. It applies to the mid-level of formality and standards of grammar, punctuation, and spelling that are used by educated people in the work-place and in school.

Nonstandard language refers to the language that is used by groups of people when speaking. It is perfectly correct in the proper situations. The key is to be able to move back and forth from the nonstandard language that we use when speaking to our friends and family members to the edited American English that is required in academic writing and in the professional areas of employment.

The following section includes words that are considered part of nonstandard language (or in a few cases, words that are used by the British but not so much by Americans) and, therefore, should not be used in academic writing.

alright—This is not a word. It is actually two words: _all right_.

a lot—This is always two words and should be avoided.

amongst—Edited American English prefers _among_. Use _among_ to compare more than two items. Use _between_ when comparing only two items.

and/or—This should be avoided when writing for the humanities. It is acceptable in certain writing for instance, legal and business writing.

anyplace—This is too informal for academic writing. Use as two words: _any place_.

can't hardly—This is nonstandard and a double negative. Use _can hardly_.

etc.—This is too informal for academic writing. Try using _and so on_.

firstly, secondly, thirdly—Edited American English uses _first, second, third_.

get into—This is nonstandard and should be avoided.

go, say—Do not use _go_ or any form of _go_ when you really mean _say_.

> And then my friend Bonnie says (not _goes_), "You better watch yourself."

good and—This is nonstandard and should be avoided.

hang out—As a verb, this is slang and should be avoided. As a noun, it is one word, _hangout_, and also should be avoided.

have to, have got to—Avoid using when you can use _have_ by itself or _must_.

irregardless—This is nonstandard. Use _regardless_ instead.

is when, is where—Do not use these words when you are defining something.

> NO: Final exam week _is when_ you are surviving on very little sleep.

> YES: Final exam week requires surviving on very little sleep.

kind of, kinda, sort of, sorta—These are nonstandard and should be avoided. Use _somewhat_ instead.

_of_—After verbs like _could, should, would, may, might_, and _must_, you should use _have_, not _of_.

> Gary could _have_ (not _of_) bought the car if he saved enough money.

off of—This is nonstandard. Use *off* on its own.

OK—This is too informal for academic writing.

reason why, the reason is because—These expressions are redundant. Use *reason* by itself, *why* by itself, or *because* by itself.

that there, them there, this here, these here—These are nonstandard. Use *that, them, this,* and *these* without *there* or *here*.

try and—This is nonstandard. Use *try to* instead.

I am going to try to (not *try and*) start my moped today.

theirself, theirselves, themself—These are nonstandard. Use *themselves* instead.

til—This is nonstandard. Use *till* or *until* instead.

EXERCISE 5.5—Correcting Nonstandard Language

Revise the following sentences that contain nonstandard language. If the sentence uses edited American English, then write "Correct."

1. Many teens fail to realize that what they put on the Internet can haunt them in anyplace for the rest of their lives.

2. Facebook and other social networking sites contain information and photos of teens that could hurt job chances for theirselves in the future.

3. Increasingly, cyber bullying ruins teens' lives in ways that should of never happened.

4. The news is full of alot of stories about teens committing suicide as a result of the pain and often public humiliation stemming from cyber bullying.

5. It seems that girls and/or young women are the targets for cyber bullying more so than boys and young men.

6. Parents and teachers have got to constantly educate teens about the risks involved in social networking.

7. Technology should be helping teens by increasing their ability to gain knowledge off of the vast World Wide Web.

8. Instead many teens lack the discipline and maturity to avoid the temptations they get into while surfing the Internet.

9. Handheld devices like tablets and of course cell phones seem like kind of an extra body part for some teens, making the Internet, video games, and social networking always part of their lives.

10. If teens were asked to avoid technology for even twenty-four hours, many would not be able to do so.

11. Pulling yourself away from technology can have positive benefits like increased concentration and appreciation for your surroundings.

12. Face-to-face communication skills amongst two people have decreased for teens who are addicted to technology.

13. Irregardless, texting brings new challenges in addition to increased communication.

14. A friend of mine will try and text her girlfriends to tell them about her latest date with her new boy-friend.

15. She texted, "I'm crazy about him," to her friend Kim, but she sent it to her new boyfriend instead.

16. This here is the reason why no one should text while drinking alcohol.

CHAPTER 6

Action

Courtesy of Margaret Steimer

EVALUATION—MAKING JUDGMENTS

Evaluation in its simplest form is a judgment about whether something is good or bad. I say, "simplest form" because our judgments are rarely simple. Critical thinking must come into all evaluating.

Critical thinking is **not** being critical about everything in the way that you are constantly disagreeing, or that there is something wrong with everything. Instead, critical thinking is the ability to look at something or some idea and really think deeply about it and question what others have to say about it.

When we evaluate, there is an automatic assumption that someone cares about our judgments. When you are evaluating for a college course, you are doing so because your audience (your peers and your professors) care about what you think. For instance, if you are asked to evaluate the orientation program at your college, your judgments are important to the college faculty and administration and potentially future students.

You are evaluating when you tell your friends about Pink's new song, and when you tell your mom what you think of her latest meatloaf recipe. Her meatloaf might not be as bad as the one she made with ground turkey, but it certainly is not as good as the one she made with cheese in it.

In order to evaluate something, you need standards. You can't judge something unless you have something to base your judgments on. When you tell your friends about Pink's latest song, you might compare it to her other songs or even compare it to Katy Perry's latest song. The truth of the matter is that **you** know what a good song is to **you**. This is based from your personal preferences for rhythm, lyrics, and the song's ability to make you want to dance.

Whether your friends agree with you or not is a different matter altogether. Some friends might think your taste in music is terrible, and others might think that you should think of becoming a professional music critic because you have such a great sense for music.

Writing evaluations requires laying out your standards that you will use to judge something and then aligning whatever it is you are evaluating to those standards. Rarely will something be **all** good or **all** bad. This is where the gray area of critical thinking lies. Not a whole lot is ever black or white. Most of the world's ideas and issues lie in the gray area somewhere in between black and white.

One way to operate in this gray area is through the use of qualifying words. Examine the two different effects of these two sentences:

Students come to college so they can party all the time.

Some students come to college so they can party most of the time.

The first sentence has the implication that **all** students go to college just so they can party. The words *some* and *most* certainly cast the statement in a fairer light. It is important that your writing uses qualifying words, so you can have a fair tone for your reader. Box 6.1 lists absolute words that can make unfair judgments and qualifying words that readers will find more reasonable.

BOX 6.1—Qualifying Words

Absolute Words	Qualifying Words
all	most, some, a few
always	occasionally, sometimes, often, frequently
every	many, several, numerous, considerable
never	once in a while, seldom, rarely

Finally, evaluation answers the question "Why?" Why is something good or bad? Your evidence for your judgments should be the best possible choices. This gathering of evidence often requires more deep thinking. Although your readers care about what you think, you should consider they are skeptics too. You have to provide sound reasoning to turn these skeptics over to your way of thinking.

For your readers to accept your evaluation, your evidence should stay aligned to your standards. Therefore, you might find yourself adjusting your standards to fit your evidence or finding more evidence to fit your standards. For instance, if you are evaluating your latest visit to a local restaurant and the service was terrible, then one standard you should use is certainly service. Do not ignore standards or evidence that might not fit the evaluation you planned on initially writing. A fair judgment covers the most important evidence and standards.

To summarize, an evaluation has the following components:

TOPIC OF EVALUATION

STANDARDS OF EVALUATION

EVIDENCE FOR EVALUATION

Prompt 6.1

Write an evaluation that judges one of the following topics. Try to operate in the gray area showing the good and bad points and using qualifying words. Choose from the following list:

Parking on campus

The service at the last restaurant where you ate

Pharmaceutical advertising on TV

Americans' attention to Great Britain's royal family

The use of a personal cell phone at work

EVALUATION—A MOVIE REVIEW

A special kind of evaluation is a movie review. You need to think of yourself as a film critic like a restaurant critic or a book critic. Dillon, a first-year student, receives the following assignment in his Media Arts class:

Movie Review

This assignment will give you practice in viewing a current movie and critiquing it thoughtfully. You may also offer your own personal insight, knowledge, and experience beyond that presented by the film's director(s).

The audience for your movie review is professors and students who will read your review to decide whether to go and see the movie, so be careful not to give away too much about the plot. You should end your movie review with a letter grade A through F (plus/minus may be used).

You will need to provide a short summary of the movie, but the majority of your writing should be an evaluation of the film. Be sure you are clear about the standards you are using in your evaluation and provide evidence from the movie to support this evaluation.

Dillon decides to go and see *Divergent*, directed by Neil Burger. What follows is the first draft of his review of *Divergent*.

Divergent: A Review

The movie *Divergent* is based on the best-selling dystopian novel for young adults with the same name written by Veronica Roth. I must admit I did not read the book, but this is probably a good thing since I would just end up comparing the book and the movie. I really liked both the movies and the books *The Hunger Games*, and I figured this story wouldn't be much different.

Divergent's setting is a run-down Chicago in the future, 100 years after a big war that the people of Chicago think has destroyed the rest of the world. There is a fence built around the city to protect this society of the remote possibility that life exists outside the boundary. The people in this city are divided into five factions based on their personality traits in order to keep the peace: Abnegation, Amity, Candor, Dauntless, and Erudite.

The Abnegation faction are the selfless people who take care of the poor and those who are factionless. Abnegation also runs the government. Amity are the farmers, and they are kind and peaceful. The people in Candor are the honest people. They never lie. The Dauntless faction are the brave ones who protect the city. They are known to be crazy and wild. Finally, the Erudite faction is the intelligent people who do all the research and medicine.

In the beginning of the movie, the main character Beatrice Prior (she later changes her name to Tris), played by Shailene Woodley, and her brother Caleb must take an aptitude test to test them to see which faction they are suited for. It's not clear how old they are, and Caleb seems to be older, and it's not clear how often the test is offered. But a lot of teenagers show up to take the test. Fortunately, each faction dresses differently, so you can tell what faction everyone belongs to.

Caleb and Tris were raised Abnegation. People in Abnegation can't even look in mirrors for very long because they reject vanity. Caleb seems to be well-suited for Abnegation, but Tris is not so sure about her future. We find out later that despite how they were raised and despite what the aptitude test says, they can choose any faction they want in a choosing ceremony. If they choose a faction that is different from the one they were raised in, they are said to be "defecting," and, as we are reminded many times in the movie, "Faction before blood." This means if they defect, they basically have to leave their family behind.

One of the problems with the film is the change in the plot. The movie is very long, two hours and twenty minutes, and the rules of the factions and the choosing of the factions seem to change too many times throughout the movie. After I saw the movie, I was curious about some of the details, so I went to the movie's website: *http://divergentthemovie.com/* . On the website, I was able to take an aptitude test, although it did not involve drinking some special serum and hallucinating because of it. I scored highest on Abnegation with Amity coming in a close second.

Tris is told that the test didn't work, and that she is "divergent." Right away, we sense that this is not a good result, as she is told not to tell anyone and is let out the back door after the test. Tris chooses a faction, and most of the movie involves how she must now test to become a full member of the faction. Again, the rules keep changing, but some of the best parts of the movie are the mental health exams she must go through to be a member of the faction she chooses.

Shailene Woodley is a great actress, and she does an awesome job in this movie. Some of her lines are unbelievably silly, for example "I don't even know who I am anymore." The character Four who ends up being like her boyfriend is played by Theo James. I believe Shailene outshines Theo James's performance, although both of them have to live with some pretty horrible lines. Another great performance is given by the outstanding Kate Winslet as the faction leader of Erudite who seeks to destroy all the Divergents and the faction Abnegation mainly because they are in charge of the government, and Erudite thinks they should be.

Another problem with the film is the fight scenes. Many of them are just not believable, and I think there are too many of them. These just add to the movie's length, which is entirely too long. Some of the special effects were awesome, especially in the mental health exams, but I cannot even compare this movie to those of *The Hunger Games*. The plots are similar, but *The Hunger Games* movies are just written better. I would give *Divergent* a grade of a C+.

Commentary of Dillon's Movie Review

1. Review the assignment requirements. What do you think are some strengths of Dillon's movie review?

2. What standards does Dillon seem to be applying to the movie review?

3. What evidence does Dillon use to support his evaluation of these standards?

4. This is Dillon's first draft. What suggestions can you offer him to improve it?

TRUSTING WHAT YOU THINK – AVOIDING PLAGIARISM

Chances are your college has an academic policy. Academic honesty is of the upmost importance for college students in this world of the Internet and all the information that can be found there. A violation of an academic honesty policy can have dire consequences including failure of a course or in the worst case, expulsion from college. Many colleges will make a notation on your college transcript as well. The bottom line is not to plagiarize; nothing is worth risking your college career.

Using sources can be tricky business, and many college students are confused by how to use sources. Blatantly using someone else's words or ideas and pretending they are yours is obviously plagiarism; however, correctly using another's words is complex. Documentation of sources requires different documentation styles, and your best strategy is to have a good handbook that covers the documentation style that you need to use for a particular writing assignment.

Documentation of sources usually requires two important components:

1. Using parentheses for citations. Different documentation styles require different formats.

2. Listing your sources in References (American Psychological Association, APA) or a Works Cited list (Modern Language Association, MLA).

It is significant to remember that **your** own thoughts are the most important part of **your** writing. Your readers want to know what you are thinking, and your thoughts should make up a large portion of most kinds of writing assignments. And of course, your thinking does not need to be documented.

Additionally, what is known as common knowledge does not need to be documented. Common knowledge is basically any fact or idea that is known by most educated people. For instance, the following statements are common knowledge and do not need to be documented.

> The earth revolves around the sun.
>
> President Barack Obama is a two-term president.
>
> Washington D.C. is the capital of the United States which is made up of fifty states.

Plagiarism occurs if ideas or words from someone else are used in your own writing without giving this person full credit. Plagiarism includes the following:

- Using a piece of writing that was written by someone other than you. This includes using a friend's paper given to you and buying a paper on the Internet. Just because you paid for a paper does not make it yours.
- Using a paper and changing it slightly. Even if the changes are significant, the ideas still belong to someone else.
- Cutting and pasting words from a source and failing to document the source correctly.
- Using ideas from anyone other than you.
- Incorrectly summarizing, paraphrasing, or quoting a source.
- Incorrectly documenting your source.

Using Sources Quiz

For the following questions, circle True or False.

1. It is possible to commit what is known as "self-plagiarism," which is reusing a writing assignment that you used for another class.

    TRUE   FALSE

2. It is possible to plagiarize unintentionally because you did not know you were plagiarizing.

    TRUE   FALSE

3. If you take someone else's words and put them in your own words, then you do not need to document the source.

    TRUE   FALSE

4. Any source found on the Internet is common knowledge; therefore, it does not need to be documented.

    TRUE   FALSE

5. Paraphrasing a source involves copying the information word for word.

    TRUE   FALSE

6. Although you did not quote from a source, you did get an idea from this source for your writing assignment, and therefore, you need to document the source.

    TRUE   FALSE

7. If you acknowledge the author of something you are quoting by naming him or her, you do not need any further documentation.

    TRUE   FALSE

8. If you find a source that states common knowledge, and you use that common knowledge in your writing, then you do not need to document the source.

    TRUE   FALSE

9. Summarizing a source involves putting the source's ideas in your own words.

    TRUE   FALSE

10. If you use what a professor in another course said in your writing assignment, then you do not need to document him or her.

    TRUE   FALSE

Avoiding Plagiarism

Avoiding plagiarism is a matter of good organization and tackling the job of incorporating your source into your writing immediately. I have seen too many times when students wait until an assignment is finished before going back to check on the incorporation of their sources. Often students then run out of time to work on their sources and their documentation, or they simply forget that they did not attend to this.

When you have a source to use in a paper you should keep the source in a separate file. Whether this file is electronic or you print the source is your decision. You should immediately summarize, paraphrase, or quote the source and document it correctly. You can try putting the summary, paraphrase, or direct quotation in large brackets or a different color or a larger font size. This way the use of the source will stand out when you are revising and editing.

Quoting, Summarizing, and Paraphrasing

You might have had teachers in your past who would encourage cutting and pasting sources into a paper. Or worse yet, students have told me about writing assignments that they have had when teachers have told them something like "You must use fifteen quotes from fifteen different sources." And the paper was only five pages long! Remember your own thinking and writing take the starring role in your writing for college. Your readers want to know what you have to say about something. Sources should be used to provide information that you did not know on your own, and therefore, the sources lend authority and credibility to your own ideas. As soon as you encounter something that someone else said or wrote and you decide to use it in your own writing, you must document it. Simply cutting and pasting from the Internet is not an acceptable practice in college and in your professional career.

Before including **any** information from a source into a paper, you have to consider these questions:

> Is the information from the source important enough to include in your paper?
>
> Did the source teach you something you did not know before coming across it?
>
> Did the source make you think differently about your topic?

If you answered "yes" to any of these questions, you should include the source information in your writing, and then you have to make the decision whether to summarize, paraphrase, or directly quote the information. Too often student writers rely on quoting rather than summarizing or paraphrasing. You should have a rationale for directly quoting. When deciding to summarize, paraphrase, or quote directly, you should consider the following:

> Is the wording and phrasing from the source technical in nature?
>
> Is the wording and phrasing from the source expressed so vividly that you would not be able to use your own words?
>
> Is the wording and phrasing from the source stated in a way that you could not possibly use your own words?
>
> If you answer "Yes" to any of the above questions, you could use a direct quote rather than a summary or paraphrase.

Quoting is a three-part process. I refer to the process as "sandwiching." The first step is to introduce who is speaking and use a signal phrase **before** the quote. Your source article does not say anything; the author of your source does. Therefore, you should avoid introducing a quote with anything like, "The article says…"

This introduction of the quotation is the bread of the sandwich and alerts your reader to expect a direct quotation. Box 6.2 has some useful verbs to use in signal phrases to incorporate your quotations, paraphrases, and summaries smoothly into your own writing. Notice that these verbs are in present tense.

BOX 6.2—Signal Verbs

agrees	explains	proves
argues	finds	recognizes
asserts	focuses on	remarks
believes	illustrates	says
claims	informs	states
comments	insists	suggests
considers	introduces	supports
demonstrates	maintains	thinks
describes	notices	writes
discusses	offers	

Next, provide the quote, using exact words, punctuation, and capitalization. Use the correct citation for the assignment. Make sure the quote is complete in terms of sentence structure. This is the meat and cheese of your sandwich. Finally, you should regain your voice by connecting the quoted material to your topic and position. Do not simply re-state the quote. This is the other slice of bread for your sandwich. Here is an example of "sandwiching":

> Tubbleman thought his meal at Liberatore's was inedible. In his review of the restaurant, he writes, "The salmon was overcooked. The vegetables were…mushy, and the salad dressing was pure vinegar" (Tubbleman 3B). Tubbleman clearly adds Liberatore's to his long list of Italian restaurants that have brought him dissatisfaction.

When deciding to summarize or paraphrase, the length of the source material is your main consideration. Both summaries and paraphrases are written in your own words and your own sentence structure. The main difference is that summaries considerably shorten the source material that you are including, while paraphrases are generally equal in length to the original. And both summaries and paraphrases still must have the required documentation to attribute these ideas to the original author.

Guidelines for Writing a Paraphrase or a Summary

Use your own words and your own sentence structure.

Avoid plagiarism. If you absolutely must quote something from the original, then you should use quotation marks around the quoted material.

Do not interpret what the author says or make a judgment about the value of the author's point. Your own opinions do not belong in a paraphrase or a summary.

Connect your paraphrase or summary smoothly into your own writing. You can use the same "sandwiching" technique that I describe above for quoting.

Use the required documentation style for your paraphrase or summary.

Additional Guidelines for a Summary

Identify the main points and condense them without losing the essence of the material. Try reading the material many times and then putting it away from you while you write the summary.

Keep your summary short.

EXERCISE 6.1—Summarizing

Read the original excerpt printed below from "A Strategic Education" by Jennifer Kalita that appeared in the last chapter. Then, read the unacceptable summary. List all the reasons the summary is unacceptable. Finally, write your own summary of the material.

Original

Step two: Think through how these skills and talents can be integrated into a more strategic approach to getting a degree that will serve you. Begin with assessing how your interests might play out in the real world. Is music the only thing that makes sense to you? If all you can think about is starting a band and hitting numero uno on the Billboard charts, think about what other coursework will support your music major. A poetry class will help you better understand how to compose good lyrics. A marketing minor will give you the skills you'll need to differentiate your band and get noticed by the big recording labels.

Unacceptable Summary

In your second step to creating a strategic education, you should think through how your talents can be integrated into a better approach to getting a degree that will interest you. Start with asking how your interests might work in the real world. Is drama the only thing that makes sense to you? If all you can think about is getting on Broadway or making it in Hollywood, you should think about what other coursework will support your drama major. An art class might help you better understand your creativity. Or you could try getting a business minor, so it will give you the skills you'll need to be different from all of the other actors and actresses out there.

"A Professor's Campaign against Plagiarism" by Kevin M. Brien

The following article was written by Kevin M. Brien, a professor of philosophy at Washington College in Chestertown, Maryland. This article originally appeared in *The Baltimore Sun* on May 4, 2013.

A PROFESSOR'S CAMPAIGN AGAINST PLAGIARISM

by Kevin M. Brien

Twenty-two years ago at the end of a semester of teaching an Intro to Philosophy course, I received an unforgettable wake-up call on the issue of plagiarism. During the reading period between the final class session and the final exam, I discovered two blatant cases of plagiarized papers—I knew the books from which these papers had been copied whole cloth. So on exam day, and with apologies to those uninvolved, I brought the issue into the open. Without naming the offenders, I told the class that I expected the students who plagiarized to meet with me privately. My deal with them: If you don't own up to the cheating, you will fail the course. If you do admit it, there will be penalties, but not necessarily a failed grade.

Imagine my dismay when twelve of the twenty-three students—half of the class—showed up, one by one, at my office door. All twelve papers did technically involve plagiarism. Five cases were deliberate and extensive; the rest involved paraphrasing of one stripe or another, sometimes with no documentation at all, other times due perhaps to ignorance of what constitutes plagiarism. Clearly, students needed more guidance in what was, to them, a murky area.

The experience was a catalyst for me to think more deeply about the issue and how I should respond. I reached out to faculty at other colleges and universities around the country asking them to share their experiences. The responses streamed back quickly, and the raw data from anonymous surveys of students concerning various forms of cheating were startling.

It seemed clear that there was a countrywide pandemic of academic dishonesty, some of it born of ignorance and some deeply ingrained in a culture of socially acceptable shortcuts. A bright spot in the surveys was how much peer affirmation of honesty discouraged cheating. But there was clear evidence that professors were generally not doing enough to promote integrity.

For the next two years I was active on my campus, working with student government and college administrators to develop awareness about the problems and to brainstorm policies that addressed them. We updated and reaffirmed the Washington College Honor Code, first established in 1976, and have continued to bolster its effectiveness in recent years. Today, our library staff teaches all first-year students about proper citation and the relationship between academic integrity and intellectual property, ideas that can prove challenging to young adults who have grown up in the "cut and paste" environment of the Internet.

Personally, I have pledged that as long as I remain active as a teacher I will never again allow myself to be complicit in cheating. At the beginning of each course I talk at length about academic integrity as a requirement of the course—a standard that I will enforce. The syllabus specifies that any written work must have an explicit honor pledge on it. For each required course paper, I distribute guidelines that include a 200-word statement about various forms of plagiarism and a notice that deliberately plagiarized papers will receive a grade of zero. Every Friday when I send students an e-mail outlining assignments for the coming week, I again remind them about signing the honor pledge on every bit of written work.

While I am not so naive as to believe that signing an honor pledge necessarily means that a given paper or exam is on the up-and-up, I make it clear to students that I refuse to have complicity in their undermining of their own education. Because I know—and I need them to understand—that by taking unethical shortcuts and not truly engaging with the material to make it their own, they are cheating themselves out of the full value of their four years here.

On a wider scale, I believe that if all faculty on every campus took a more proactive, ongoing stance to encourage academic honesty, it would go a long way in cultivating a positive ethos of integrity in all of our students and, ultimately, in our society. We all know that there is a dark abyss of dishonesty in much of the business world, much of the political world and much of everyday life.

Imagine a countrywide shift in our academies to actively counter the negative ethos of academic dishonesty. Could this not gradually generate a shift to a positive ethos of integrity, not only in academic work, but in all aspects of our lives and our everyday dealings with one another? Is not integrity one of the qualities of a good citizen? And is it not the responsibility of a good teacher to cultivate an ethos of integrity in the classroom and beyond?   9

Reaction to Writing

1. If you do not know the meanings of the following words, try to determine their meaning from the surrounding context in Brien's article. Check their meanings in a dictionary and write a sentence using each word.

   blatant (1)

   catalyst (3)

   pandemic (4)

   affirmation (4)

   complicit (6)

   undermining (7)

   ethos (8)

   abyss (8)

2. Other than the ideas that Brien presents, what are other ways professors can discourage plagiarism?

3. Answer the three questions that Brien asks in his last paragraph.

VERBS

Verbs are perhaps the most important part of speech. Do you remember from Chapter 2 that the basic sentence is comprised of the subject and the predicate? Verbs occupy the predicate of a sentence, while nouns and pronouns occupy the subject. Verbs tell the action that is happening for the subject or link the subject to another word or words that describe it (these are called linking verbs).

Anthony <u>cooks</u> like a professional. (*Cooks* describes the action of Anthony.)

Anthony <u>is</u> an excellent chef. (*Is* links Anthony to the description of him.)

Verbs have many tenses. For just two examples, present tense verbs describe actions happening right now (bring, catch, dance, forget), and past tense verbs describe actions that happened in the past (brought, caught, danced, forgot).

Strong writers use strong action verbs. Table 6.1 lists some strong action verbs in present tense that you can try to use in your own writing. If you don't know the definitions of these verbs, you should consult a dictionary to increase your vocabulary.

TABLE 6.1   Strong Action Verbs

accelerate	command	distribute	implement	perfect	smash
accomplish	communicate	document	impose	persevere	solidify
achieve	comply	educate	improvise	pioneer	specify
acquire	conceive	elevate	infuse	polish	sponsor
adapt	condense	eliminate	initiate	predict	standardize
administer	conduct	employ	inspire	prioritize	streamline
alert	conserve	empower	instill	produce	strengthen
analyze	consolidate	encourage	integrate	propose	structure
anticipate	contribute	enforce	interpret	recognize	struggle
appraise	control	enhance	invent	rectify	summarize
approve	convene	enrich	investigate	reevaluate	support
assemble	convert	ensure	isolate	regulate	tailor
assert	coordinate	escalate	lecture	rehabilitate	target
assess	counsel	exceed	leverage	reinforce	terminate
augment	critique	execute	maintain	renew	tighten
automate	cultivate	exploit	maneuver	represent	translate
avert	decrease	fabricate	manipulate	research	transmit
balance	dedicate	facilitate	master	resolve	travel
bolster	demolish	familiarize	mentor	restructure	triple
calculate	demonstrate	focus	modify	retrieve	unify
capitalize	devote	forecast	motivate	revitalize	unite
centralize	devour	formulate	navigate	revive	upgrade
certify	diagnose	fortify	negotiate	salvage	validate
challenge	discipline	govern	orchestrate	scorch	vanquish
clarify	discover	guard	organize	seize	verify
collaborate	dispatch	illustrate	participate	shield	wield

EXERCISE 6.2

Choose ten strong verbs from Table 6.1 that you are unfamiliar with or that you use rarely in your own writing. Consult a dictionary to get their definitions. Then write an original sentence using each word.

The senses (look, smell, sound, taste, and feel) when used as verbs can function as linking verbs.

> He looked tired.
> She felt happy.
> The laundry smelled fresh.

Linking verbs also include forms of the *be* verb (*am, was, is, are*) and other verbs that have a sense of being or becoming (*seem, grow, turn, stay, remain*).

Verbs often provide the new information for the reader in a sentence. They are instrumental in maintaining the continuing momentum of writing.

> VERBS   occupy the predicate
>
> show the action
>
> link to the subject to describe it
>
> move your writing forward

For these reasons, verbs are extremely important in our writing. Unfortunately, they also cause writers the most problems. The two main problems writers have with verbs are agreement and tense.

Subject Verb Agreement

Verbs are said to be singular or plural depending on whether the subject is singular or plural. We refer to this grammar rule as "number." "Agreement" occurs when a singular subject agrees with a singular verb and when a plural subject agrees with a plural verb.

> The *boy runs* very fast for his age. (singular subject and verb)
> The *boys run* very fast for their age. (plural subject and verb)

Most of the time, we can rely on instinct from our speaking to choose the correct verb to agree with the subject. The challenge writers have with agreement might stem from the simple notion that we realize to make a noun plural we usually add an *s*. However, it is just the opposite for verbs. The singular verbs are the ones in many cases that have the ending *s*.

In addition to number, verbs also follow the concept of "person" or "point-of-view." First-person singular refers to the writer or "I." Second-person point-of-view refers to your readers, whom you are writing to. Third-person point-of-view refers to what or whom you are writing about.

	Singular	**Plural**
First-person	I *run*.	We *run*.
Second-person	You *run*.	You *run*.
Third-person	He, She, It, or a singular noun *runs*.	They or plural nouns *run*.

Some verbs do not follow the rule of adding an ending *s* to make them singular in the third-person point-of-view. These verbs are said to be "irregular" because they do not follow the regular pattern. Below are the patterns for the irregular verbs "to be," "to have," and "to do."

"to be"	**Singular**	**Plural**
First-person	I *am*.	We *are*.
Second-person	You *are*.	You *are*.
Third-person	He, She, It, or a singular noun *is*.	They or plural nouns *are*.

"to have"	**Singular**	**Plural**
First-person	I *have*.	We *have*.
Second-person	You *have*.	You *have*.
Third-person	He, She, It, or a singular noun *has*.	They or plural nouns *have*.

"to do"	**Singular**	**Plural**
First-person	I *do*.	We *do*.
Second-person	You *do*.	You *do*.
Third-person	He, She, It, or a singular noun *does*.	They or plural nouns *do*.

Photo courtesy of James G. and Elizabeth R. Troutman

EXERCISE 6.3

Circle the correct verb form in the following paragraphs.

Many people (realizes / realize) that elephants (has / have) good memories, but the largest mammal walking on Earth also can communicate with one other and with humans. Much research (goes / go) into studying elephants, and researchers (has / have) determined that elephants (responds / respond) to human voices and hand signals like waving hello.

Elephants (is / are) now endangered, and humans (is / are) their number one predator. In the late 1970s, there were 1.3 million African elephants. Now it is estimated that only 500,000 elephants (is / are) left. Kenya (is / are) passing stronger laws to protect its elephants. Unfortunately, China (continues / continue) to hunt elephants for their ivory which is used in Chinese artwork and religious icons.

These gentle giants (is / are) shot by powerful automatic weapons all for their tusks. Now, technology like a Global Positioning System (GPS) (is / are) being used to protect elephants. Also, if an elephant (is / are) known to be at risk for its tusks, protectors will tranquilize it and (removes / remove) the tusk as a preemptive tactic. The bottom line is there is only a finite supply of ivory from elephants.

We (knows / know) that elephants are maternal, and they (has / have) family units. They also (mourns / mourn) their dead which is becoming more and more common with the threat of poachers. Fortunately, the elephants also protect themselves by understanding human voices and knowing that men (is / are) their biggest threat.

Challenges with subject verb agreement occur for writers during the following circumstances:

1. The subject and verb are separated by prepositional phrases or dependent clauses.

2. The subject is a compound subject which makes the subject and verb plural.

3. The verb comes before the subject in a sentence.

4. The subject is an indefinite pronoun, meaning it is difficult to determine whether it is singular or plural.

5. The subject is a collective noun or an organization, making it difficult to determine whether it is singular or plural.

1. Prepositional phrases are formed with a preposition and a noun or pronoun. The noun or the pronoun is the object of the prepositional phrase. The prepositional phrases are italicized in the following sentences:

For lunch, Matt had his leftover chili *from dinner.*

Debbie stayed *at the bar* too late *on Saturday* to hear her favorite band.

I must remember to mail my stepmother's birthday present *to her* tomorrow.

When prepositional phrases separate subjects from verbs, writers can have problems with agreement.

The roster *of clients' names and mailing addresses* was updated to include their e-mail addresses. (*Was* agrees with *roster* **not** *names and addresses.*)

Jane *in her winter coat and boots* walks carefully on her icy driveway to get to her car. (*Walks* agrees with *Jane* **not** *coat and boots.*)

Another form of an interruption between the subject and the verb is the dependent clause. Do you remember the first discussion of dependent clauses in Chapter 3? Table 3.2 has some of the words that are used to create dependent clauses. Most of the time these dependent clauses are formed with relative pronouns (*that, who, whose, whom,* and *which*). When dependent clauses separate subjects from their verbs, writers can also have problems with agreement.

My cousins *who love the beach* travel rarely to the Atlantic Ocean. (*Travel* agrees with *cousins* **not** *beach.*)

The old Ferrari *that has had many owners* is now a historic car. (*Is* agrees with *Ferrari* **not** *owners.*)

EXERCISE 6.4

Cross out the prepositional phrase and dependent clauses that separate the subject from the predicate in the following sentences. Circle the correct verb form.

1. The increase in the use and marketing of what are known as e-cigarettes (has / have) caused concern for parents.

2. These battery-operated devices which operate with liquid nicotine (burns / burn) without producing the offending smell and second-hand smoke.

3. An e-cigarette though not as widely used as regular tobacco cigarettes (is / are) now seen as cool by young people.

4. A teen who wants to hide smoking from his or her parents (inhales / inhale) the liquid nicotine without having to worry about the smell of smoke.

5. These devices that are available in a disposable or refillable form (is / are) found in many convenience stores.

6. Smoking e-cigarettes with the vapor that is produced (is / are) more accurately called "vaping" and the e-cigarettes are called vaporizers.

7. Vaping with its high-strength concentrates (is / are) being looked into by the Food and Drug Administration (FDA).

8. Little scientific research about e-cigarettes (creates / create) more concern among parents and doctors.

9. It is already known that the liquid nicotine with its elevated levels (causes / cause) serious consequences if ingested rather than inhaled.

10. The battery itself in vaporizers with its electronic circuitry being used so close to developing brains (provides / provide) another area of concern.

11. The debate about e-cigarettes or vaporizers (continues / continue) as more studies are conducted about their effects.

12. The FDA will most likely (bans / ban) e-cigarette sales to minors.

2.   A compound subject has two or more subjects. These subjects are only connected by *and*, *or*, and *nor* to make a subject compound. Subjects are **not** made compound with any of the following phrases: *as well as*, *in addition to*, *such as*, *including*, *together with*, *along with*, and other similar phrases. Compound subjects using *and* are plural and require plural verbs. In the case of compound subjects connected with *or* and *nor*, the subject closest to the verb is used to determine agreement. If the subject after *or* and *nor* is singular, then the verb will take a singular form. If the subject after *or* and *nor* is plural, then the verb will take a plural form.

The high school student and his parents are greeted by the admissions staff at the college. (*Student and parents* require the plural verb form *are.*)

The high school student as well as his parents is greeted by the admissions staff at the college. (*Student as well as parents* require the singular verb form *is.*)

The hotel or its stores have an employee theft problem. (*Stores* is closer to the verb, requiring the plural verb form *have.*)

The sorority sisters nor the sorority house mother is at the house on weekends. (*Mother* is closer to the verb, requiring the singular verb form *is.*)

3.   Sometimes a verb comes before its subject in a sentence. The most common way this happens is due to the structures *there is*, *there are*, *there were*, *here is*, *here are*, and *here were*. In these cases the subject follows the verb.

There are many problems with spring registration this year. (The subject is *problems*, requiring the plural verb form *are.*)

Sometimes a verb comes before its subject because a prepositional phrase starts the sentence.

> Across the hall from the English seminar are the art classes. (The subject is *classes*, **not** *seminar*, requiring the plural verb form *are*.)

It helps to invert the sentence to see the agreement more clearly.

> The art classes are across the hall from the English seminar.

You will see the subject following the verb in questions also. It helps to answer the question to see the subject verb agreement.

> Where *are* my car keys? My car keys *are*…

> Who *is* my roommate next year? My roommate next year *is*…

4. Indefinite pronouns refer to pronouns that stand in for non-specific nouns, and these pronouns are often difficult to judge whether they are singular or plural. Table 6.2 lists the most common indefinite pronouns.

TABLE 6.2 Indefinite Pronouns		
always singular	always plural	sometimes singular/ sometimes plural depending on context
another	both	all
anybody	few	any
anyone	many	more
anything	several	most
each		some
either		none
every		
everybody		
everyone		
everything		
much		
neither		
nobody		
no one		
nothing		
one		
somebody		
someone		
something		

You certainly do not need to memorize this table. A good way to test to see if an indefinite pronoun is singular or plural is by matching it with the singular verb form *is* and the plural verb form *are*. For example, do you say "everyone is" or "everyone are"? Chances are you can instinctively hear that *everyone* takes a singular verb form.

You cannot use this test for the indefinite pronouns that depend on the context, or the surrounding sentence, to determine whether they take a singular or plural verb form (*all, any, more, most, some*, and *none*).

> None of the students have their homework completed. (*None* is referring to the plural noun *students*, requiring the plural verb form *have*.)

> Most of the yard work is finished for the weekend. (*Most* is referring to the singular noun *work*, requiring the singular verb form *is*.)

> Most of the groceries that I bought last week have been eaten. (*Most* is referring to the plural noun *groceries*, requiring the plural verb form *have*.)

Indefinite pronouns will be discussed again in Chapter 7 where sexist language is discussed.

5.   If the subject of a sentence is a collective noun then it is sometimes difficult to determine the correct subject verb agreement. Collective nouns are generally singular when they refer to a group of people acting as one unit. Sometimes collective nouns are plural when the members of the group are acting as individuals. In determining correct subject verb agreement for collective nouns, a writer must look at the context of the sentence. Box 6.3 shows some common collective nouns.

BOX 6.3

Common Collective Nouns			
family	audience	class	number
committee	team	group	staff
faculty	herd	jury	college
company	crowd	government	society
*media			

Media is the plural form of *medium*. For instance, television is one type of medium where we get our news. When it is used to mean a group of journalists and broadcasters or to mean many medium sources such as newspapers, magazines, television, and movies, it is considered singular.

To test whether a collective noun is singular or plural, requiring a singular or plural verb form, try using the words *separately* and *combined* after the collective noun.

> The committee (*separately*) cast votes in the election. (In *committee* the members are acting individually to place their votes, requiring the plural verb form *cast*.)

> The women's swim team (*combined*) wins the state championships every year. (In *team* the members are acting as a unit, requiring the singular verb form *wins*.)

The media (*combined*) has a strange fascination with celebrities. (In *media* the members, journalists, and broadcasters, are acting as a unit, requiring the singular verb form *has*.)

Finally, if a named organization or a titled publication is the subject, the verb form is singular.

Tips for Breaking into the Stock Market is an excellent reference for the new investor.

Jericho, Kahill, and Vetters, attorneys of law, is the best law firm I know.

Additionally, if a singular noun ends with *s*, the verb form is singular.

The news is filled with so much violence these days. (Although *news* ends with an *s*, it is a singular noun, requiring the singular verb form *is*.)

EXERCISE 6.5

Circle the correct verb form in the following sentences.

1. The pictures that you take of yourself with your cell phone (is / are) now called "selfies."

2. These days everyone from little kids to President Obama (takes / take) selfies of themselves.

3. It was seen at the great leader of South Africa Nelson Mandela's funeral that First Lady Michelle Obama looked on disapprovingly as President Obama along with Britain's Prime Minister David Cameron and Denmark's Prime Minister Helle Thorning Schmidt (snaps / snap) selfies of themselves.

4. It turns out there (was / were) reasons for Michelle Obama's disapproval.

5. The sign language translator with his bizarre facial expressions and fake signings (appears / appear) to be in a trance.

6. There (is / are) evidence now that he was.

7. When the 2013 World Series winners the Boston Red Sox visited the White House, the selfie that player David Ortiz (takes / take) of himself with President Obama (goes / go) viral online quickly.

8. After this selfie, everyone at the White House (has / have) been discouraging any more selfies with President Obama.

9. A selfie such as those pictures of President Obama (is / are) relatively harmless unless it becomes a matter of privacy.

EXERCISE 6.6

Brian was a college freshman in his second semester when he wrote this. Find and correct his fifteen subject verb agreement errors.

When I decided to go to college, and I actually was accepted, I knew I was in for a huge adjustment. In high school, the teachers and the staff treats us like babies. My mother who is raising my twin baby sisters insisted that I am ready because I earned good grades in high school. However, I knew in high school everybody were looking out for me and the other students. On any given day, my science teacher or my Advanced Placement tutors updates me on what is due. All of the classes whether English, Spanish or Math is the same. The teachers collect assignments as late as a month, and they are always reminding us when everything is due. They even lets us redo work if it was a low grade.

My family hope for the very best for my college career because college cost major money. There were so much pressure on me when I started my freshman year. It didn't help that I almost failed out during my first semester. My mother nor my professors was any help. The problem was I had no time management skills.

In college, there is so many distractions. I found my grades slipping when I spent way too much time playing video games with my friends. And nobody were there to tell me to do my work. I had to develop responsibility for myself and my schoolwork.

By October, I decided I needed to get organized when I saw my dismal midterm grades. Scheduling appointments and deadlines in a planner as well as organizing all of my notes and assignments were the first things I did. I knew studying has to come first before I can watch movies with my friends. I even sent my video games home. Learning to manage my time and organizing due dates in my planner is still hard for me, but I managed to come back for a second semester. The book my mother gave me for my high school graduation *College Success in Ten Steps* help me every day as well. I can't wait to make her proud when I graduate in four years. No one have ever graduated from college in my family. I want to be the first!

Verb Tense

Verbs change tenses to show time, when an action occurred. For some tenses, helping verbs of *have*, *be*, and *will* are used. The three simple verb tenses are present tense, past tense, and future tense. The future tense requires the helping verb *will*.

Present Tense:	Don loves football.
Past Tense:	Don loved football.
Future Tense:	Don will love football.

Earlier you read about regular verbs and irregular verbs where irregular verbs are said to be "irregular" because they do not follow the regular pattern. The verb *love* is a regular verb as it takes the *–ed* ending for all past tense forms.

"to love"	past tense	Singular	Plural
First-person		I *loved.*	We *loved.*
Second-person		You *loved.*	You *loved.*
Third-person		He, She, It, or a singular noun *loved.*	They or plural nouns *loved.*

The verb *be* is said to be irregular because it does not follow the regular patterns for tenses.

"to be"	past tense	Singular	Plural
First-person		I *was.*	We *were.*
Second-person		You *were.*	You *were.*
Third-person		He, She, It, or a singular noun *was.*	They or plural nouns *were.*

EXERCISE 6.7

Complete the blanks with the correct present or past tense form of the verb *be*.

I _____ one of the few people who lives at the beach and does not like the beach. I have some friends who _____ like me but not many. If my niece and I go to the beach we _____ under a beach umbrella which might or might not withstand the strong wind.

The sand and the seagulls _____ particularly annoying. At one beachside restaurant I go to, the servers wear only socks on their feet so when they _____ serving drinks and food on the beach, their feet don't burn. In addition, all sorts of other dangers _____ in the sand including broken glass, cigarette butts, and pesky creatures like sand fleas and little sand crabs. This past summer, my friend Holly _____ on the beach and all of the sand fleas must have been hungry because they _____ biting everyone.

Seagulls _____ what I call flying ocean rats. In my lifetime, I have had seagulls swarming me many times. When people have food, especially Boardwalk® fries, the seagulls _____ right there to steal them. Over the years, it seems seagulls have grown in size. They certainly have plenty to eat between human's food and their ocean diet. Additionally, there _____ always the danger of seagull droppings landing on you when you least expect it.

The ocean scenery _____ peaceful, but in the height of summer when beach blankets _____ covering most of the beach and the tourist season _____ in full swing, a "local" can easily wish summer to end.

Regular verbs all use the same past tense *–ed* form when they are used as past participles. Past participles are used with helping verbs for other tenses. Sometimes the –ed ending is dropped when we speak, so it is important that you include it in your writing.

NO: I was suppose to wash the car.

YES: I was supposed to wash the car.

Table 6.3 lists some common irregular verbs with their past tense form and past participle.

TABLE 6.3   Common Irregular Verbs

Tense		Past Participle	Tense		Past Participle
Present	Past		Present	Past	
be (is, am, are)	was, were	been	keep	kept	kept
beat	beat	beaten	know	knew	known
become	became	become	lay	laid	laid
bite	bit	bitten or bit	leave	left	left
break	broke	broken	let	let	let
bring	brought	brought	lie	lay	lain
build	built	built	light	lighted or lit	lighted or lit
buy	bought	bought	lose	lost	lost
catch	caught	caught	make	made	made
choose	chose	chosen	mean	meant	meant
come	came	come	ring	rang	rung
cost	cost	cost	run	ran	run
cut	cut	cut	say	said	said
deal	dealt	dealt	see	saw	seen
dig	dug	dug	send	sent	sent
do	did	done	set	sets	set
draw	drew	drawn	shake	shook	shaken
drink	drank	drunk	shoot	shot	shot
drive	drove	driven	show	showed	shown or showed
eat	ate	eaten	sing	sang	sung
fall	fell	fallen	sink	sank or sunk	sunk
feed	fed	fed	sit	sat	sat
feel	felt	felt	sleep	slept	slept
fight	fought	fought	speak	spoke	spoken
find	found	found	spend	spent	spent
fly	flew	flown	spin	spun	spun
forget	forgot	forgotten or forgot	stand	stood	stood
forgive	forgave	forgiven	steal	stole	stolen
freeze	froze	frozen	sting	stung	stung
get	got	got or gotten	stink	stank or stunk	stunk
give	gave	given	sweep	swept	swept
go	went	gone	swim	swam	swum
grow	grew	grown	swing	swung	swung
hang	hung	hung	take	took	taken
have	had	had	tell	told	told
hear	heard	heard	think	thought	thought
hide	hid	hidden	wear	wore	worn
hit	hit	hit	write	wrote	written
hurt	hurt	hurt			

Two other verb tenses include present perfect tense and past perfect tense. Writers do not need to know these terms necessarily, but it is important to be able to use these tenses correctly in your writing. The present perfect tense requires the helping verb *has* or *have* added to a past participle. The present perfect tense is used when an action occurred in the past and is still occurring or it ended at a specific time in the past.

Present Perfect Tense:	Don *has loved* football all of his life. (This tense shows that Don's love of football occurred in the past and is still occurring.)
Present Perfect Tense:	I *have loved* football.

The past perfect tense requires the helping verb *had* with a past participle. The past perfect tense is when an action occurred in the past and ended before some other past action.

Past Perfect Tense:	Don *had loved* football until his love of baseball started. (This tense is used to show that something happened in the past and ended before some other past action.)

It is important to remember to use simple past tense for events that happened in the past and to use past perfect tense for events that happened before another past event. No helping verbs are needed for simple past tense.

Kim *had gone* before we *arrived*. (*Had gone* is past perfect tense and *arrived* is simple past tense.)

Progressive tenses are used to describe an ongoing action, a habitual action, or a continuing condition. The present progressive tense uses the present tense form of the verb *be* that agrees with the subject's number and person with the *–ing* form of a verb.

Present Progressive Tense:	Halle *is washing* her car.
Present Progressive Tense:	We *are taking* our time with our taxes this year.

The past progressive tense uses the past tense form of the verb *be* that agrees with the subject's number and person with the *–ing* form of a verb.

Past Progressive Tense:	I *was going* to the drycleaner every week in the month of January.
Past Progressive Tense:	They *were joining* friends to watch the New York Giants play the Dallas Cowboys.

What's Not a Verb?

While you are thinking about verbs, you should also be reminded that words can look like verbs, but they are not functioning as verbs in the sentence. For instance, the word *walk* can be a noun as in this sentence:

I am going to take a long walk.

If you add *–ing* to *walk* and form *walking* you can make an adjective or another noun.

Don't forget to bring your walking stick on our hike.
Walking is a great way to clear your mind.

When you have what looks like a verb, you can't make the assumption that it is one, unless it is functioning as a verb in a sentence. The *–ing* form of verbs is especially tricky. Consider this sentence:

Running back and forth in the fenced yard, the dog was excited to see his owners return home.

The simple predicate in this sentence is *was*. *Running back and forth* is a phrase that modifies the dog. Verbs in the *–ing* form and in what is called the infinitive form which is *to* and the simple present tense of a verb like *to walk* are often modifying phrases.

The advocates to prevent child abuse are planning a 5K run in May.

The phrase *to prevent child abuse* modifies *advocates*. The predicate in this sentence is *are planning*, and it is in present progressive tense.

One final word on verb tense deals with simple present tense. Always make sure that you use simple present tense when you are making a statement that continues to be true, for instance with people's names.

NO:	What did he say his name was?
YES:	What did he say his name is?
NO:	His name was Rick Johnson.
YES:	His name is Rick Johnson.

EXERCISE 6.8

Circle the correct verb form in the following sentences.

1. Celebrities with all of the saturated media coverage that they receive (provides / provide) many examples of naming their kids with the oddest choices.

2. In the 1960s, Frank Zappa (made / had made) people notice when he (named / had named) his first child, a daughter, Moon Unit.

3. Moon Unit Zappa (followed / was followed) by the arrival of her younger brother in 1969.

4. Her brother's name (is / was) Dweezil.

5. Many people laugh when they (hear / had heard) George Foreman, a retired boxer, grill inventor, and father of twelve, named his five sons all George.

6. Apple (is / was) the name of the actress Gwyneth Paltrow and the band Coldplay's member Chris Martin's daughter.

7. In 2002, Michael Jackson (has / had) a strange idea when he named his youngest son Blanket.

8. Actually, both of Michael Jackson's sons' legal names (is / are) Prince Michael Jackson I and II.

9. His daughter (is known / was known) by simply Paris Jackson, but she (is named / was named) Paris-Michael Jackson.

10. Paris Hilton, a socialite and celebrity according to some, (is / was) an heiress to the Hilton Hotel fortune.

11. Actress Angelina Jolie and actor Brad Pitt (has adopted / have adopted) children from around the world and (has had / have had) children in the traditional way too.

12. They have a daughter named Shiloh and a son who (is named / was named) Knox, the same as Fort Knox where the United States (stores / store) its gold reserves.

13. In the constant search for creative names, actor Tom Cruise and actress Katie Holmes (has / had) an interesting idea with their daughter's name Suri.

14. American rapper Jay-Z, whose legal name is Shawn Corey Carter, and American R&B singer Beyoncé unsuccessfully (tried / have tried) to trademark their daughter's name Blue Ivy.

15. Most recently, celebrity Kim Kardashian and singer and record producer Kanye West (welcomed / have welcomed) daughter North West in June 2013.

THE WRITING PROCESS—EDITING

Editing is the last step of the writing process, and you should try to resist editing until after your revising is complete. While revising attends to the larger structural issues like organization, editing attends to all the little fixes. If you would handwrite something, editing would be when you make sure all your i's are dotted and your t's are crossed. Before the wonderful world of computers, writers were stuck using typewriters. Editing would be a painful process of looking for typos. Typos occur now with word processing, but fixing them is so much easier. In fact, your computer can be a big help with editing.

Professional writers have editors to help them catch "little" mistakes. Although "little," these mistakes can have a big impact on your reader. You wouldn't want to have readers judge you as careless or worse, not very smart, by having them read through a mess of misspelled words and fragments. If you can find someone else to read your writing that would be a huge help for both revising and editing. If your campus has a writing center, you might want to consider going there to seek the help of a writing center tutor. Writing centers can provide a lot of help with every step of the writing process. Don't think that they are "fix-it" shops; they're not. However, writing center tutors can offer you those fresh set of eyes that are so necessary for writers. And the best thing about writing center help is it's free!

Having your writing read by someone else creates the most important part of the writing situation—audience. You are not writing in a vacuum. Someone will ultimately be reading your writing. And if the writing is for a grade, you cannot afford to skip revising and editing. Even more will be at stake when you are writing for work. I have heard many stories about people being turned down for promotions due to poor writing skills.

You will find that for different assignments you will use different techniques to edit. When you are ready to edit, try some of these techniques.

Consider printing whatever it is you're working on in order to work with a printed copy. It's easier to find errors on a printed copy than on a computer screen.

Read your work aloud **slowly** to catch areas where you are missing a word and to find commonly confused words that your grammar-checking and spell-checking software does not find.

Try reading your writing backwards to spot errors. Read the last sentence and then the next to last and so on. This way you won't be so focused on content.

Try using a ruler to keep yourself focused on one line at a time.

If you are trying to edit on the computer screen, you can try to enlarge the font size to make it easier to find errors. Or you can highlight two or three sentences at a time and then keep moving the highlighting.

Try to keep a "problems log" where you keep track of your own problems that you know you have with your writing and that others have pointed out to you in the past.

Checklist for Evaluating Your Paragraph

○ I have a clear, confident **topic sentence** that states my main point.

○ I use **details** such as sensory details, examples, names, numbers, specifics, and evidence to support my main point.

○ My supporting details are arranged in a **logical order**.

○ I use transitional expressions, repetition, pronouns, and parallelism to create **coherence**.

○ My concluding sentence reminds readers of my main point and makes an observation.

○ Everything discussed in my paragraph refers back to my main point to maintain **unity**.

○ All sentences are complete, consisting of a subject and a predicate, making independent clauses.

○ I have no run-ons, nor comma splices.

○ I use semicolons correctly and sparingly.

○ I use commas correctly.

○ I have avoided nonstandard and texting language.

○ I have correct capitalization.

○ I use strong verbs that agree with their subjects and are in the correct verb tense.

○ My paragraph is formatted correctly per the assignment's instructions.

- My headings are double-spaced in the left-hand corner.
- If required, my title is centered and capitalized properly. My title is neither underlined nor italicized, and it is in the same font and font size as the rest of my writing. My title is meaningful and original.
- My first sentence is indented and the text is double-spaced.

CHAPTER 7
Change

Photo courtesy of James G. and Elizabeth R. Troutman

WRITING THE ACADEMIC ESSAY

"Prose is architecture, not interior decoration."

Ernest Hemingway

So far we have been focusing on paragraphs as independent units. You might have been frustrated to move on to full essays, and that is exactly what we are now going to do. The academic essay is nothing to fear and nothing to loathe. All of the purposes (describing, narrating, illustrating, analyzing, and evaluating) that you used for your paragraphs remain the same. Now these paragraphs become the mainstay of your essay.

Quite simply, an essay has three parts: an introduction, the body, and a conclusion. Your body paragraphs will still have topic sentences to begin each of them. Each body paragraph will explore one main point. Two main questions surface about these body paragraphs:

1. How long should each paragraph be?

2. How many body paragraphs do you need?

1. Your paragraph development for an essay is the same as the development of stand-alone paragraphs. Your topic sentence is your guide for the main point that you want to cover in a paragraph. The lengths of paragraphs vary depending on how involved this main point is. You make a promise to your reader to fully cover the main point that you reveal in your topic sentence. Therefore, your reader expects the main point to be explained thoroughly in the paragraph. Your reader also expects to have paragraph breaks. No paragraph should be longer than three-quarters (75%) of a full double-spaced page. If you need additional length to fully develop a main point, you should use transitions to split the paragraph to a length that is more manageable for your reader.

2. Different essays require a different number of body paragraphs. You might be familiar with a five-paragraph essay. This essay follows the following structure:

paragraph 1:   introduction

paragraph 2:   first body paragraph covering first main point

paragraph 3:   second body paragraph covering second main point

paragraph 4:   third body paragraph covering third main point

paragraph 5:   conclusion

The five-paragraph essay is an attempt to give writers an enforced structure so that they have to focus only on content. In other words, the form is already provided, all you have to do is fill the form with your ideas. A problem with the five-paragraph essay is that not all essays have three main points. Some essays have five or six main points, and some might have only two. You have to use your good judgment to use the **best** reasons and evidence to develop an essay. Obviously, if your instructor requires a certain number of paragraphs, then you need to follow the assignment guidelines. However, if you have the opportunity to provide as many paragraphs or as few paragraphs that you want, then you should have a rationale when planning your organization and structure of an essay.

Creating a Working Thesis Statement

A thesis statement works similarly to a topic sentence in many ways:

> Both are focused and make a specific point.
>
> Both provide a position about your specific point.
>
> Both can be justified (explained or proven) in the writing that remains. For a topic sentence, the paragraph's length is sufficient for this explanation. For a thesis statement, the essay's length is sufficient for this explanation.
>
> Both are strong.

While topic sentences begin body paragraphs, the thesis statement is found in the introduction. Often, professors prefer your thesis statement to be the last sentence of the introduction. You should always check with your professor about his or her guidelines.

The thesis statement focuses your entire essay. Sometimes it also gives your reader a sense of the structure or development of your essay. For example, for an essay evaluating the dog breed known as pit bulls, a student writer Colleen formulates the following working thesis statement:

> Although pit bulls often get a bad rap, they actually make good pets because of their intelligence, patience with young children, and ease for training.

After reading this thesis statement, a reader expects the three reasons—intelligence, patience with young children, and ease for training—to be covered in the essay in that **same** order. One way to move from a topic to a working thesis statement is to ask a question about the topic and then when you answer it, the answer could form your working thesis statement. In developing her working thesis statement, Colleen asked, "Why should people consider getting a pit bull as a pet despite the bad rap they get?"

I call your thesis statement a **working** thesis statement because you should expect to change your thesis statement as you draft. While writing her essay about pit bulls, Colleen develops another reason that pit bulls make good pets: they are highly lovable. She revises her thesis statement to include this reason:

> Although pit bulls often get a bad rap, they actually make good pets because they are intelligent, patient with young children, easy to train, and highly lovable.

Notice that Colleen changed the structure of her thesis statement from all noun phrases (intelligence, patience, and ease) to adjectives (intelligent, patient, easy, and lovable). She did this because she could not think of a way to make "highly lovable" parallel with the noun phrases, so to create parallelism, she revised the sentence structure.

Writing Introductions

You are always introducing yourself to lots of people: new roommates, classmates, professors, and maybe even employers and customers. Just like the introductions that we make with people in person, our introductions in writing have to let the reader know who you are as the writer. And just like in our face-to-face introductions, you want to make a good impression because your reader might be your boss, a potential date, or, as is the case in the college classroom, your professor.

A good introduction has four components:

1. It makes a good impression by being interesting and original.

2. It makes a "promise" to the readers as to what they can expect when they read the rest of your writing.

3. It informs your reader of your topic and purpose for writing.

4. It shows who you are in terms of your position about the topic.

An introduction is often called the "hook." The idea behind this is that you are hooking your readers' interest to make them want to read further. You can do this in many different ways:

○ Tell a story from your own personal experience that relates to your topic and thesis.
○ Use a vivid example, providing lots of sensory details.
○ Ask a question. You might even consider asking the question that brought you to your thesis statement.
○ Find a simple way to explain something complex.
○ Describe a situation that connects to your topic and thesis.

Your position about your topic will be apparent from your thesis statement. Try not to be too mysterious in your introduction. Often writers want to create a sense of suspense with their introductions. In other words a writer is saying to the reader, "Yes, I know you have no idea where my essay is going from this introduction. But you will just have to read the whole essay in order to find out." This is not an effective approach for your introductions of academic essays. Sometimes a straightforward approach is your best strategy for certain writing situations.

Another ineffective introduction is the one that goes a bit like this, "According to *Webster's Dictionary*…" Your readers most likely know the definition of the word that you are defining, so they will find this kind of introduction insulting. This is just another example of what I call throat-clearing. Readers suspect that you are using a stalling tactic, perhaps because you have no idea how to start, and they will not be interested in reading much further. Additionally, the introduction is not the place for you to figure out what it is you want to say. The introduction is all about your reader. It is not a place for you to find a way into your topic.

If you have are having problems writing your introduction, don't worry. Many writers find themselves not quite sure how to start. The important thing is that you have a working thesis statement to give a focus to your essay. You can begin by developing your body paragraphs. In drafting these, you will probably come across a way to write your introduction. You need to start somewhere, and if you find yourself beginning with the body paragraphs, that is fine. Your thinking about your topic and position about your topic develops as you write. Writers do not have all of their ideas in their heads, as if all they have to do is some sort of "brain dump." You have to write to uncover your thinking about the topic. This is why sometimes your true ideas are not uncovered until you write a page or two. If this happens, you can go back and revise your working thesis statement and introduction to match what it is you're truly saying.

Carissa Scaniffe was born in Maryland in 1990. She wrote this poem when she was a freshman at James M. Bennett High School, in 2004. Now Carissa is a single mom and works in the hotel industry. She says that she considers herself a life-long writer as she often writes poetry, song lyrics, and short stories.

WHY ARE THE SKIES BLUE? BY CARISSA SCANIFFE

Why are the skies blue—why do we have to go to school?

Why is there so much violence—and some children have to live in silence?

Why can people be so mean—and be so different than what they seem?

Why do children grow up not believing—and have those friends who are deceiving?

Why don't people dream anymore—and there is always someone criticizing the poor?

When will all of the war nonsense stop—and the police do their jobs and just be good cops?

When will people choose to be who they are—and realize that not everyone is meant to be a star?

When will the Earth stop spinning—don't you wish sometimes you could start from the beginning?

When will children in other countries know fun—and what it would be like to play out in the sun?

Will the world ever change—or will it just stay the same?

Reaction to Writing

What question that Carissa raises seems to be the most relevant to you? Why?

Prompt 7.1

Write a short essay, using your own personal experience that addresses one of the themes raised by Scaniffe in her poem "Why Are the Skies Blue?"

CAUSE AND EFFECT—ANALYZING CONSEQUENCES

© 2014 Stuart Miles. Used under license from Shutterstock, Inc.

We look at causes and effects daily in our lives. If someone is unhappy with you, you do some soul searching to find what specifically caused the effect of unhappiness. If you stayed up way too late last night, you are feeling the effects of lack of sleep. Cause and effect essays can take your writing in one of three ways:

You can look at the causes of some particular effect. OR

You can look at the effects of some particular cause. OR

You can look at both the causes and the effects. (You will probably want to look at the causes first.) Often causes and effects are a chain reaction.

something CAUSES something else which CAUSES something else

Writing about causes and effects is another type of analysis, covered in Chapter 5. It requires deep thinking as you look for causes and effects that are not the most obvious ones. What is the point for your audience to read a causal analysis if you reveal no new information?

Often a causal analysis takes the form of asking why.

Why is traffic backed up at this same place every weekday morning? (looking for CAUSES)

Why is medicinal marijuana being legalized in most states? (looking for EFFECTS)

Why is there so much school violence? (looking at CAUSES and EFFECTS)

Causal analyses are often quite complex because related events spread out to other related events. For instance, if you look at school violence, then you will see that the causes and effects intertwine fairly quickly in your analysis. This overlap of related events causes writers many challenges. Often, the writing gets messy in the drafting stage before the real topic and analysis is discovered.

When you analyze causes and effects, there are generally four components:

1. You must **identify** all the causes and effects that you can.

2. You must **interpret** the relationships among the causes and effects.

3. You must **evaluate** the significance of these relationships.

4. You must **debate** their importance.

A problem that writers encounter in writing a causal analysis includes faulty correlation. This is the murky area of stating that because something happened before something else, then that first happening must be the cause of the second. Superstitions work like this. Because you broke a mirror this morning then this must be the reason you failed your math exam. This "chicken and egg" syndrome (which came first, the chicken or the egg?) can cause any writer headaches. This is why a causal analysis needs careful examination and a thoughtful evaluation.

Another problem that comes up in writing about causes and effects is overgeneralizations. Overgeneralizations are especially noticeable as writers set out to look at societal issues. It is so easy to blame "society" for societal issues. Additionally, the media is often a scapegoat for everything in our culture. Consider the following example.

The "Hookup" Culture among Young People

The "Hookup" culture is a frequent topic in the media when it comes to millennial college students. The term "hooking up" refers to college students, many of whom are complete strangers to one another, kissing and having sex casually outside the boundaries of dating or a real relationship. The media portrays this culture as prevalent across college campuses in America. But is this really the case?

It helps in looking at a phenomenon closely to use visuals like arrows between causes and effects, or a table with causes on one side and effects on the other. In completing the following table, try to avoid using "media" or "society" as a cause for the "hookup" culture.

EXERCISE 7.1—CAUSES AND EFFECTS OF THE "HOOKUP" CULTURE

Complete the following table. It might prove interesting to pair up with someone of the opposite sex to complete this exercise.

Causes	Effects

Many ideas probably came from this exercise especially if you were able to discuss it as a class. Now in pursuit of writing an essay about this, frequently one cause or one effect might strike you as more interesting than the others. For example, let's say "peer pressure" was named as one cause of the "hookup" culture. You probably have a position about whether peer pressure contributes to this "hookup" culture that the media seems to insist is so common among the younger generation. Your position will lead you to your thesis statement.

Your narrowed topic + Your position about this narrowed topic = Your thesis statement

All of the constant talking among college students about hooking up creates the idea that everyone is doing it.

Remember a thesis statement remains a working thesis statement until your essay is truly finished. Now you can develop your ideas about the "constant talking" about hooking up, and at the same time, you can reject other causes.

Organizing Your Ideas

A causal analysis essay like **all** other essays incorporate many of the purposes used in this textbook (describing, narrating, illustrating, analyzing, and evaluating). For instance, when you write your introduction, you might have to describe the event that you are analyzing in order to provide background for your readers. Or, you could narrate a story to give your readers a sense of the phenomenon or event you are analyzing.

The body paragraphs of your essay should be focused on your own ideas about your narrowed topic. You will want to have sharp details still using S.E.N.S.E. (sensory details, examples, names and numbers, specifics, and examples). You want your readers to understand not only what it is you see about the narrowed topic, but also why you see it and why they should see it too. Again, you can not successfully write **any** essay unless you avoid the obvious.

Causal analyses often follow an order of importance where your most important cause or effect is last. This is often the case if you are analyzing many causes or many effects, or if you are presenting causes or effects and rejecting them one by one until you reach the one you think is most important. Finally, as you conclude your essay, resist the temptation to summarize unless your analysis is lengthy or especially complex. You definitely want to emphasize the importance of what you have to say.

Prompt 7.2

Write a causal analysis essay using the skills discussed in this chapter. Choose one of the following prompts that you care about and you have personal experience with in order to communicate your own ideas. Remember you will need to discover a narrowed topic and thesis statement suitable for a double-spaced, two to three paged essay.

- ○ Your ideas generated from Exercise 7.1
- ○ Look in your college or local newspaper for an event that you can add ideas to by looking at the causes and effects of this event
- ○ A controversial trend among your peers

"FONFI"

In 2013, *The Oxford Dictionary* added FOMO to its online dictionary. FOMO means "Fear Of Missing Out." FOMO could be a real compulsive disorder when someone has stress and anxiety for fear of missing out on something, often an opportunity for a great social experience or interaction. However, it is most often attributed to social media. People experience FOMO when they see posts on social media about an event they are missing out on.   1

Although perhaps even clumsier than the term FOMO, I would like to add another term: FONFI or "Fear Of Not Fitting In." Many people have claimed that college students today fear not fitting in. If they go away to college, especially a fairly long distance from home, then they encounter other students who are so different from themselves, often for the first time in their lives. Not only are these the typical differences one would expect—ethnicity, sexual orientation, and religion—but also one other difference that is not as expected. Students have varying levels of education at college just like in high school and sometimes even more varied than in high school.   2

College should have a sense of community or of "belonging" for everyone. However, this sense of not belonging or fear of not fitting in is quite prevalent in college especially among women and minorities. For some students, there is the fear of being "dumber" than everyone else. For others, there is an equal fear of **revealing** that they are smarter than many of their peers.   3

This fear of not fitting in has consequences. For the brighter students, they can fall into the trap of dumbing down themselves in order to fit in. These students actually find college and its coursework underwhelming. For the students who think they are as dumb as first graders, they lack the confidence that they need to succeed, and often they put so much pressure on themselves, it hinders their learning.   4

College students focus too much on what others think of them. They need to use college for one of its intentions: finding out who they really are. Students need to be themselves and allow themselves to develop their own identities. They care so much about making connections with friends and having constant communication with this network of friends that they often miss out on developing themselves and cultivating satisfying relationships.   5

So often I have heard from college students that they form their circle of friends at college in the first few days of college. Many of these friendships last beyond college, even a lifetime. However, some others are quickly forgotten when students transfer schools or graduate. I wonder, are they truly authentic friendships or a symptom of the fear of not fitting in? Worse even than having a fake friendship, would be students who become chameleons, those lizards that change their colors to match their surroundings, whatever it takes just to fit in.   6

Reaction to Writing

1. The title is "FONFI." What is the purpose of using a made-up word for an essay's title?

2. If you do not know the meanings of the following words, try to determine their meaning from the surrounding context in the article. Check their meanings in a dictionary and write a sentence using each word.

compulsive (1)

ethnicity (2)

prevalent (3)

underwhelming (4)

hinders (4)

cultivating (5)

authentic (6)

3. What is the effect of the discussion of FOMO in the first paragraph and not FONFI? Is it effective? Why or why not?

4. The word *revealing* is bolded in paragraph 3. Why do you suppose it's bolded?

5. Do you believe college students have FONFI? Why or why not?

6. What are some other consequences of having FONFI that are not discussed in the article?

PRONOUNS—AGREEMENT

Pronouns take the place of nouns and pronouns that are close to them. *He, she, it, they, their,* and *your* are all pronouns. Without pronouns our writing would be quite tedious and repetitive.

> Bonnie could not refuse Jim's request. Bonnie knew that Jim would continue to ask Bonnie out if Bonnie did not agree to go out with Jim.

> Bonnie could not refuse Jim's request. She knew that he would continue to ask her out if she did not agree to go out with him.

The noun that the pronoun is standing in for is called an **antecedent**.

> **Tom** could not find glasses that **he** liked. (*Tom* is the antecedent for the pronoun *he*.)

There are many kinds of pronouns. Box 7.1 lists the personal pronouns that stand in for people and things.

BOX 7.1

Personal Pronouns				
I	you	she	he	it
me		her	him	
we		they		
us		them		

Possessive pronouns show ownership. Box 7.2 lists the possessive pronouns.

BOX 7.2

Possessive Pronouns			
my	your	hers	its
mine	yours	his	
our		their	
ours		theirs	

Pronouns are either singular or plural in number. In Chapter 6, you were introduced to the indefinite pronouns in the discussion of subject verb agreement. Table 7.1 shows the indefinite pronouns and whether they are singular or plural.

TABLE 7.1 Indefinite Pronouns		
always singular	always plural	sometimes singular/ sometimes plural depending on context
another anybody anyone anything each either every everybody everyone everything much neither nobody no one nothing one somebody someone something	both few many several	all any more most some none

EXERCISE 7.2—Identifying Pronouns

Circle or highlight all of the personal, possessive, and indefinite pronouns in the following paragraph written by Melanie, a first-year student.

Everyone has people who have helped them throughout their lives. I would not be in college writing this paper if it were not for my boyfriend Alex. Alex has supported me in every step I have taken since last winter. I did not plan on coming to college, even though it was my dream to leave Long Island. The plan was to stay home, go to community college and help raise my two younger brothers in order to make everyone else happy. Honestly, I was not happy with that plan. Alex knew that it was time for me to put myself first. There was not a day that he did not remind me to do something for myself. Putting everyone first was always my priority even if I was not content with doing it. Alex helped me make my dream come true by supporting me when I decided to apply to college out of state. The day I read my acceptance letter, I knew that no one in my family would be truly happy for me to attend college, and it broke my heart. Over time, my heart was healed because Alex defended my decision every step of the way. Eventually, everyone realized that it was time to put myself first, and they suddenly became supportive of me furthering my education. Who knew with Alex's help that my life would change forever? I am proud to say going away to college was the best choice I have ever made, and I give Alex all of my love and gratitude.

In addition to number, pronouns also follow the concept of person or point-of-view. First-person point-of-view refers to the writer. This is where you have heard the first-person pronoun "I." Second-person point-of-view refers to your readers, whom you are writing to. Third-person point-of-view refers to what or whom you are writing about.

First-Person: *I* can understand his opinion.

Second-Person: *You* can understand his opinion.

Third-Person: *They* can understand his opinion.

Singular pronouns that stand in for people also indicate gender: *he* or *she*, *him* or *her*, and *his or hers*.

Pronoun Antecedent Agreement

Pronouns must agree with their antecedents in terms of number (singular or plural), person (first-, second-, or third-person), and gender (male or female). Some of the rules about pronoun antecedent agreement might sound familiar to you because they are similar to the rules of subject verb agreement. However, unlike subject verb agreement where the subject and verb are both in the same sentence, pronoun antecedent agreement causes problems for writers because often the pronoun is in a sentence or two after its antecedent. Or the pronoun's antecedent can not be found because it is assumed. After completing Exercise 7.3, you will see what I mean.

EXERCISE 7.3—Identifying Pronouns and Their Antecendents

Circle or highlight all of the personal, possessive, and indefinite pronouns and underline their antecedents (what the pronouns are standing in for) in the following paragraph found earlier in this chapter.

In 2013, *The Oxford Dictionary* added FOMO to its online dictionary. FOMO means "Fear Of Missing Out." FOMO could be a real compulsive disorder when someone has stress and anxiety for fear of missing out on something, often an opportunity for a great social experience or interaction. However, it is most often attributed to social media. People experience FOMO when they see posts on social media about an event they are missing out on.

Many times, writers take advantage of the flexibility of pronouns and this causes problems with agreement. When we write, our tendency is to think of one reader for our writing. For this reason, we lean towards singular pronouns. This creates a problem with pronoun antecedent agreement.

NO: A college student should be able to choose their advisor. (*Student* is singular and the pronoun *their* is plural.)

YES: A college student should be able to choose an advisor.

YES: College students should be able to choose their advisors.

YES: A college student should be able to choose his or her advisor.

Many, many years ago, half of the population—females—was left out of written text. The singular pronoun automatically was *he, him,* and *his.* Today, this is considered sexist language. We have to have our pronouns agree with their antecedents in terms of number in our writing. You will notice that this does not apply to informal speaking or even most speaking it seems, as you will hear plural pronouns being matched to singular antecedents all of the time, especially on television.

To fix the disagreement between plural pronouns and singular antecedents, you have four options described in Box 7.3.

BOX 7.3

Four Ways to Fix Sexist Language and Pronoun Antecedent Disagreement

Sexist: Every attorney has ten minutes for his summation.

Option 1: All attorneys have ten minutes for their summations.
(Use a plural noun and a plural pronoun.)
(Make sure all words in the sentence are made plural.)

Option 2: Attorneys have ten minutes for summations.
(Omit pronoun entirely.)

Option 3: Every attorney has ten minutes for a summation.
(Use an article—*a, an, the*—instead of a pronoun.)

Option 4: Every attorney has ten minutes for his or her summation.
(Use *his or her* to make the singular pronoun to the singular noun.)

*** NOTE: *One* is a singular indefinite pronoun, and generally is not used as a personal pronoun in America.

NO: One only needs to listen to one's own thinking.

YES: A person only needs to listen to his or her own thinking.

Option one is the most effective approach, whereas option four is the least effective approach because it can get quite cumbersome in writing. Notice also that option four does not use a slash as in *his/her*. This is not considered acceptable in academic writing. You should write out *he or she*, *him or her*, and *his or her*. Also, sometimes option two and option three are not options because the sentence structure will not allow for omitting the pronoun or using an article instead of the pronoun.

These same four options can be used to maintain pronoun antecedent agreement for the indefinite pronouns (see Table 7.1). Do you remember the test from Chapter 6 used to determine whether an indefinite pronoun is singular or plural? A good way to test to see if an indefinite pronoun is singular or plural is by matching it with the singular verb form *is* and the plural verb form *are*. For example, do you say "everyone is" or "everyone are"? Chances are you can instinctively hear that *everyone* takes a singular verb form, and the pronouns that are used for the antecedent *everyone* should also be singular.

*** NOTE: *Everyone* is a singular indefinite pronoun as one word. *Every one* is two words when your meaning is each part of a whole.

> *Everyone* enjoyed *every one* of the flavored cheesecakes at our wedding.

You can not use this test of *is* or *are* for the indefinite pronouns that depend on the context, or the surrounding sentence, to determine whether they are singular or plural (*all*, *any*, *more*, *most*, *some*, and *none*).

> *None* of the students have *their* homework completed. (*None* is referring to the plural noun *students*, requiring the plural pronoun *their*.)

> When packing luggage for vacation, *most* is packed at the last minute with *its* contents overflowing. (*Most* is referring to the singular noun *luggage*, requiring the singular pronoun *its*.)

Collective nouns name groups of people or things. Collective nouns are generally singular when they refer to a group of people acting as one unit. Sometimes collective nouns are plural when the members of the group are acting as individuals. In determining correct pronoun antecedent agreement for collective nouns, a writer must look at the context of the sentence. Box 7.4 shows some common collective nouns.

BOX 7.4

Common Collective Nouns			
family	audience	class	number
committee	team	group	staff
faculty	herd	jury	college
company	crowd	government	society
*media			

Media is the plural form of *medium*. For instance, television is one type of medium where we get our news. When it is used to mean a group of journalists and broadcasters or to mean many medium sources such as newspapers, magazines, television, and movies, it is considered singular.

To test whether a collective noun is singular or plural, requiring a singular or plural pronoun, try using the words *separately* and *combined* after the collective noun.

> The *family* (*combined*) is spending *its* vacation in Fripp Island, South Carolina. (*Family* is operating as a singular unit, requiring the singular pronoun *its*.)

> My *company* (*separately*) left my dinner party after midnight, rushing to *their* cars in the cold air. (*Company* is operating as individuals, requiring the plural pronoun *their*.)

EXERCISE 7.4—Fixing Pronoun Antecedent Disagreement

The following sentences were written in response to the essay "FONFI" found earlier in this chapter. Revise each one, so there is no problem with disagreement between pronouns and their antecedents and there is no sexist language. Refer to Box 7.3 for help.

1. If a person can't be who they really are, then they will live their entire life as a lie.

2. No one wants to stand out, and no one wants their own sense of identity.

3. Everyone has equal rights no matter if they look like they belong or not.

4. I think everybody, even if just for a short time, has felt like they don't belong.

5. There is no reason that someone so young should be unhappy in their own skin and definitely not because someone else made them feel that way.

6. Someone coming to college with an unusual background should do all they can do to fit in.

7. The media makes girls become someone they are not just to fit in.

8. Everyone should listen to the Dove® campaign and "Love the skin they're in."

9. Young males seem to have fewer problems than young females in being content with who he is.

10. Fitting in is what our society dictates to be their standard.

CHAPTER 8
Balance

COMPARE AND CONTRAST—MAKING DECISIONS

As adults, we are always making decisions from what we are going to eat for breakfast in the morning to how we are going to dress for the day. Many of these decisions stem from comparing many items to choose one. In writing, we often compare two or more topics to show similarities, and we contrast two or more topics to show differences.

NOTE: When you compare two things, you use the word *between*. When you compare three or more things, you use the word *among*.

I could not decide *between* chocolate ice cream and strawberry.

I could not decide *among* my many choices what to eat for lunch at the mall's food court.

As an example, you can compare and contrast two television crime shows, two political candidates, or two NASCAR® drivers to an interested audience.

For the purpose of this discussion, I will use the words *compare* and *comparing* to mean to show similarities and differences since the words *compare* and *contrast* are so closely linked. When choosing two topics to compare, your reader is crucial to this decision. It makes little sense to compare two subjects that have obvious similarities and differences. For instance in the following example, you can see the difficulty the student writer faces when comparing men and women.

A Poor Example

Male and Female Differences

Who is more dominant a man or a woman? Many people say that men are, but then others say women are more dominant. Who really knows who is more dominant? Because no matter what, both genders are discriminated against. No doubt about it there has always been striking differences between men and women. Women have battled society since day one. Men were looked at as the dominant sex, and women were looked at as the weaker sex who cleans, tends to their children, and serves dinner to their families. The fact that men and women are different is well known.

Men are considered to be physically stronger than women. You rarely see women working at construction sites or other "manly" jobs. Men are always the strong ones physically but when it comes to mentally, women always hold that title. While it may be true that men are stronger physically, women are stronger than men psychologically. Most women have better communication skills than some men. Another case of a psychological difference is reaction to stress. Men tend to react violently; women react by communicating in a friendly way. Men keep things inside them and pull away from others, while most women talk about things that are bothering them. Men and women are different in many ways, communication skills, cognitive skills, body structure and strength. After all we are born to be different, and to have different roles in this world.

This writer has little hope in saving this attempt at an essay. Choosing a topic that matters to the reader is important, so is the scope of the comparison. You have space and time constraints in writing a compare and contrast essay. Hundreds and hundreds of books have been written about the differences between men and women. If you are writing a two-paged essay, you would have to narrow your topic significantly. For example, look at the following narrowing process:

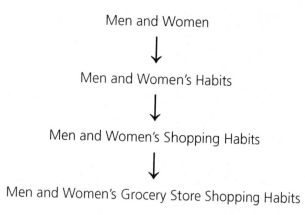

Men and Women

↓

Men and Women's Habits

↓

Men and Women's Shopping Habits

↓

Men and Women's Grocery Store Shopping Habits

Now, assuming the student writer has personal experience and examples to draw from, this narrowed topic might work for a two-paged essay, and it might interest the reader.

Finally, when choosing subjects to compare, you should choose from the same groupings. Why would you compare a housefly with say, a tulip? That comparison is completely ridiculous. It would make much more sense to compare a housefly to some other flying pest like a mosquito, assuming you have a reason to do so.

In choosing subjects to compare, you should observe four principles:

1. Avoid subjects that have obvious similarities and differences. Your reader will not be interested, and you will have an unmanageable mess.

2. Choose comparisons that matter to the reader.

3. Narrow your topics considerably, allowing for space and time constraints.

4. Choose subjects that are from the same group.

To compare and contrast subjects seems relatively straightforward. However, much thought has to go into not only the selection of subjects, but also to the purpose for comparing. Remember that your purpose is not to compare two subjects because you were told to do so. Your consideration of your reader is important here too. You can ask yourself the following questions to help clarify your purpose for writing a comparison:

○ Do you want to **explain** the similarities and differences to your reader because they are not easily apparent?

○ Do you want to **evaluate** the strengths and weaknesses of two subjects to your readers because they need to make a decision with this information?

○ Do you want to **describe** the advantages and disadvantages of two subjects to your readers because you will make the decision, and you need to persuade your reader that it's the correct one?

NOTE: You generally want to use the words *advantages* and *disadvantages*, *strengths* and *weaknesses*, or *similarities* and *differences*. The words *pros* and *cons* are considered slang.

You can see this double method of writing requires considerable thought. Even more thought is required in regards to organization. When you compare two subjects, you need to find points of comparison. For example, Julie has to write a compare and contrast essay for her writing class, and she has to take calculus next semester for her nursing major. She decides to compare the two professors at her college who teach calculus, Dr. Gabriel and Dr. Barrett. In deciding which professor's course to take, she talked to many students who have had calculus with either Dr. Gabriel or Dr. Barrett. Knowing that she is going to struggle with the course, Julie chooses three points of comparison: the professors' teaching method, their availability for help outside of class, and the difficulty of their exams.

She can organize her essay with two methods: subject-by-subject or point-by-point. Subject-by-subject comparisons are ideal for shorter essays or a short comparison in a longer essay. This pattern has its drawbacks in that it can make your essay divided in half which might put a strain on your reader's memory. The reader has to first read all about one subject and then has to read all about the second subject.

Point-by-point comparisons are usually for longer essays and are ideal when the points of comparison are important. However, with this method, the reader can easily get lost in the details and might have difficulty seeing the subjects as a whole. The following outlines show how the two methods would work with Julie's comparison.

Subject-by-subject	**Point-by-point**
Dr. Gabriel	teaching method
teaching method	Dr. Gabriel
availability outside of class	Dr. Barrett
difficulty of exams	availability outside of class
Dr. Barrett	Dr. Gabriel
teaching method	Dr. Barrett
availability outside of class	difficulty of exams
difficulty of exams	Dr. Gabriel
	Dr. Barrett

In addition to organizational patterns, writers have to think about emphasis. Will one subject get more of an emphasis than the other? Will one point of comparison have more emphasis than the others? Will differences get more of an emphasis than similarities? Emphasis matters for your purpose and your thesis statement. Because Julie is writing her compare and contrast essay for the real purpose of choosing between two professors, she first has to take a close look at what the previous students of the two professors had to say. She decides on the following thesis statement:

> Although Dr. Gabriel's exams are more difficult, her availability for help outside of class and her teaching method is preferable over Dr. Barrett's.

Julie considers that perhaps other students who need to take calculus at her college will be interested in reading her comparison. She thinks of these readers as she drafts her essay.

The thesis statement for a compare and contrast essay should show the points of comparison and might make an evaluation. This returns us to the idea of purpose. In brainstorming and drafting this kind of essay, writers might find that an outline or some other organizational tool is helpful.

Prompt 8.1

Write a double-spaced, two paged compare and contrast essay using the skills covered here on one of the following topics. Your intended audience is your professors and classmates. In your thesis statement, you will include at least three points of comparison and make an evaluation similarly to how Julie did in the above example.

You can make the decisions about emphasis and which organizational pattern you choose to use. Make sure you consider what information your readers need to know about the subjects you are comparing. This background information should be included in your introduction.

Two part-time jobs you have had or are considering

Two magazines of the same type (for example, *Time* and *Newsweek*)

The advertisements on two different websites

Two chores (one that is difficult and one that is easy)

Two brands of cereal

DEVELOPING BODY PARAGRAPHS

A frequent complaint that I hear from my fellow writing professors is that students need to be able to develop their ideas more deeply, and they need to be specific and detailed about those ideas. So often students might skip all planning and brainstorming and jump right into the drafting of the essay—all in an effort to just get the writing done. The writing, however, will happen more easily if some planning is done that requires some deep thought about the topic.

Let's look at an example. Students in a first-year writing class were asked to write a short essay about an event that changed their lives. They were told to use the compare and contrast method to describe who they were before the event and who they were after the event.

One student named Susan thought about it for awhile and decided to write about when her younger brother was diagnosed with cancer. She decided on the following working thesis statement:

After my brother was diagnosed with cancer, it changed my outlook on life.

After deciding on a topic and developing a working thesis statement, the problem Susan then encountered was she couldn't come up with any more ideas other than her specific topic. She started to worry about how she was ever going to fill two whole pages.

Susan is not alone. Students often decide on a topic and maybe even a position about that topic, and then they freeze. You might have had this situation happen to you. One idea that Susan's professor encouraged her to try is to interview herself with the journalistic questions: Who? What? When? Where? Why? How? The trick here is not to answer the questions simply. You need to fully flesh out the answers and maybe use one or two particular journalistic questions, for example "how?" more than once. Susan's list of questions looked like the following:

Who was involved when Jimmy was diagnosed with cancer? Describe all these people and Jimmy.

What kind of cancer was it? What were his symptoms?

When did this happen in my life and Jimmy's life?

Where was I when I was told?

Why did this affect me so much?

How did this affect me?

The last two questions really created a lot of material. Susan's professor then reminded the class that the assignment required them to describe the event and describe who they were before and after the event using the compare and contrast method. Susan created even more material to use in her drafting when she explored who she was before Jimmy's cancer diagnosis, and who she was after it. She also realized that her working thesis statement needed to be revised. The part about "it changed my outlook on life" was so general. She thought deeply about two more questions:

What is my outlook on life?

How has my outlook on life changed?

The idea behind fully answering these questions that you pose to yourself is to gather enough material (even too much would be good) from your deep thinking **before** you set out to draft. You can then lay out all of your ideas to discover your main points from all the material you gathered. Once you discover the main points of all this material, you can organize them in an order where you cover each main point in a paragraph.

You can now turn each main point into a topic sentence to start a paragraph. You then provide the evidence and examples that support the topic sentence. Try to write quickly to get all the information down. You can look at the flow and specific wording later when you revise. Use all the specifics that support each topic sentence. If your paragraphs seem to become too long, don't worry. You can always divide paragraphs using a reasonable approach when you revise.

Using Specific Words

Similar to having well-developed paragraphs that reveal deep thinking, good writers use specific words and avoid vague or general words that provide little information to their readers. Box 8.1 illustrates some of these vague or general words that you should try to avoid in your writing.

BOX 8.1

Vague Words		
a lot	issue(s)	sort(s)
aspect(s)	kind(s)	stuff
awesome	nice	thing(s)
bad	OK	today's society
factor(s)	situation	very
good	society	whatever

Developing a strong vocabulary should be a goal of all college-educated adults. This is developed through a natural curiosity about words and through reading. Make it a goal to broaden your vocabulary by keeping track of new words and by using a dictionary and a thesaurus.

THE WRITING PROCESS—PEER REVIEW

A part of the revising and editing steps in the writing process should be peer review. You might be familiar with this process, but you should not think of your peer as an editor who is responsible for finding all of your errors, for example, comma splices, and fixing them for you. Just like going to a writing center tutor, peer review should be about having a real reader interested in the success of your ideas coming across in your writing. Peer review is **not** peer editing.

Ideally, you will have an opportunity to have a classmate in the same writing class with the same assignment review your writing. A classmate will be familiar with the coursework, your professor, and the assignment's expectations. Peer review should be a meaningful and beneficial way to improve your writing. It is not a way to waste precious class time, nor is it something that should make you defensive. You do not have to follow any of the advice your peer reviewer has for you.

You will want to have a printed, finished first draft for your peer reviewer. At the same time that you are having your draft reviewed, you will be reviewing your classmate's draft. Here are some ideas to consider when you are reading his or her paper:

1. You should read slowly with a pen in hand. While reading, mark whatever you want on the paper: places that need explanation, confusing sentence structure, areas that need qualifying (try to use *some* instead of *every*), and particularly effective language that you want to point out. Remember the writer is still revising and editing the essay (it's still a draft), so you want to make sure the writer doesn't delete what you found as effective.

2. Introduction: After reading the title and the introduction, stop reading. How interested are you in continuing to read? What are your expectations for the rest of the essay? Jot these down along with suggestions you have for the writer to improve the introduction.

3. Thesis: Is the writer's thesis statement somewhere in the introduction or if your professor requires it, is it at the end of the first paragraph? Does the topic seem narrow enough for the assignment? What is the author's position about the topic? How original and meaningful is the thesis? At this point, you might want to check with the author that you have identified the thesis statement. If you have, continue reading. If you are unsure about your classmate's thesis, you might want to offer suggestions to make it clearer and then continue reading the rest of the essay.

4. Support for thesis: Is the thesis adequately supported? Has the author proven his or her thesis? How specific are the examples? What examples can you think of to add?

5. Personal experience: How does the writer use his or her own personal experiences? Is it effective? Why or why not? Remember everyone has something significant to say. Help your classmate find this significance.

6. Clarity: Are there any parts that are unclear? Are there any places that you need more background? Make sure you point these out to the writer.

7. Reading comprehension: Are there any parts that you had to read and re-read and maybe you still don't understand? Can you identify the cause of this problem? Faulty sentence structure? Strange phrasing or weird word choices?

8. Transitions: Are the transitions between sentences and paragraphs adequate? What can be done to improve the writer's forward progression from one point to the next? Remember the essay should be smooth reading and not bumpy.

9. Conclusion: Do you have a sense of completion or does the essay just end? What works and doesn't work about the conclusion? If you find yourself wanting more from this essay, can you identify what it is?

10. Write at least five sentences about your ideas to help improve your partner's paper. Give this back to the writer along with the draft containing your other comments.

11. As time allows, discuss your comments and make sure you thank one another for helping each other improve your drafts.

PRONOUNS – CASE AND REFERENCE

In addition to person and number, pronouns have what is known as case. Case refers to what form the pronoun takes. Pronouns have three different cases: subjective (the pronoun is the subject of the sentence), objective (the pronoun is an object or an object of a phrase), and possessive (the pronoun indicates ownership). Possessive pronouns were covered in the last chapter, however Box 8.2 shows all three of the pronoun cases.

BOX 8.2

	Pronoun Case		
	Subjective	**Objective**	**Possessive**
First-person singular	I	me	my, mine
First-person plural	we	us	our, ours
Second-person singular and plural	you	you	your, yours
Third-person singular	he, she, it, who, whoever	him, her, it, whom, whomever	his, her, hers, its, whose
Third-person plural	they, who, whoever	them, whom, whomever	whose, their theirs

Subjective Pronouns

Many of you might remember when you were younger, a similar scenario to the one below:

A son says to his mother: "Jimmy and me are going to the park." OR "Me and Jimmy are going to the park."

The mother corrects her son: "Jimmy and I are going to the park."

In this scenario, the mother is correcting the pronoun case of her son. The first-person singular pronoun in the subjective case is *I*, and pronouns always come at the end of compound subjects that contain nouns. And *I* is always last.

NO: Barb, I, and he went to the bank.

YES: Barb, he, and I went to the bank.

Objective Pronouns

Pronouns in the objective case function as objects and objects of prepositional phrases. Direct objects receive the action of the verb.

We walked *her* to her car because it was so late at night. (*Her* is the direct object of *walked*.)

I gave the bouquet of roses to *her* for her birthday. (*Her* is the object of the preposition *to*, completing the prepositional phrase.)

Compound Subjective Pronouns and Compound Objective Pronouns

Writers encounter problems when pronouns become compound, connected with *and, or,* and *nor,* with other pronouns and nouns.

My brother and *I* [not *me*] went shopping. (Ignore "my brother and" to know that *I went shopping* is correct.)

Give the check to my dad or *me* [not *I*]. (Ignore "my dad or" to know that *Give the check to me* is correct.)

The preposition *between* seems to cause the most problems for writers and speakers too, for that matter.

NO: The argument between Sam and *I* will never end. (The preposition *between* requires the objective case, not the subjective case *I*.)

YES: The argument between Sam and *me* will never end.

TIP: To help remember this rule, I like to think that *between* with its *ee* sound matches *me* with the same sound.

When you want to emphasize a noun by using a pronoun with it, the pronoun should be in the subjective case if the noun is operating as the subject and the objective case if the noun is operating as an object.

NO: *Us* ladies are going to the restroom.

YES: *We* ladies are going to the restroom.

NO: Give all of the credit to *he* the true hero.

YES: Give all of the credit to *him* the true hero.

Possessive Pronouns

Writers often have confusion with the possessive pronouns because possessive nouns take apostrophes and possessive pronouns do not.

NO: *Our's* is the only team left from Pennsylvania in the playoffs.

YES: *Ours* is the only team left from Pennsylvania in the playoffs.

Also, the third-person singular possessive pronoun is *its* not *it's*, which is the contraction of *it is*.

NO: The cat liked to sleep in *it's* basket.

YES: The cat liked to sleep in *its* basket.

EXERCISE 8.1

Revise the following sentences to fix problems with pronoun case. If the sentence is correct, write "Correct."

1. I and my sister go to the mall shopping because we have the same clothing style.

2. The issue about the missing money brought out mistrust and jealousy between my girlfriend and I.

3. Most girls are seen as sensitive in most situations, and boys are supposed to be strong, but when it comes to my brother and I, its the other way around.

4. When I was growing up, the chores around the house were usually my mom's and I job.

5. After Christmas, my sister and me got into a big dispute about the number of gifts we received.

6. It seems hard for my girlfriend and I to juggle time among extracurricular activities, school work, and friends.

7. Many boys were nurtured to one day be the man of the house, so us boys have to understand that the girls are often seen as the little princesses who get their way.

8. When you are finished with dinner, please save the leftovers for Frank and I.

9. Please keep that private information between you and me.

10. Me and my friend both want to be lifeguards this summer.

11. Several organizations had fundraisers in the spring, but their's was not one of them.

12. If only my sister and him could make a decision, we could proceed with the new addition for the house.

13. Andrew complained that text messages for his roommate and he were getting quite lengthy.

14. There are two cars in our driveway; we had ours and the Bakers had their's.

15. We wondered whether the boss and him would support our new proposal.

Reaction to Cartoon

1. What is the pronoun error in the cartoon above?

2. Why would the cartoonist intentionally have this error in his cartoon?

3. Try to determine the meaning of *predilection* from the surrounding context. Check its meaning in a dictionary. What is a synonym for *predilection*?

4. What is the effect of the penguin Joe using the word *predilection* **and** having a pronoun error?

Pronouns with Linking Verbs

Remember from Chapter 6 that linking verbs are verbs that do not show action. They show a state of being or a condition. Linking verbs are the forms of the verb *be* (*am, is, are, was, were, have been, had been*), verbs that describe the senses (*look, sound, taste, smell, feel*), and verbs that describe a sense of being or becoming (*seem, grow, turn, stay, remain*). When pronouns follow linking verbs, the pronouns rename the subject of the sentence, so they should be in the subjective case.

An easy way to remember this is to flip the sentence. The pronoun should work as the subject. For example, try flipping the second sentence to determine the correct pronoun:

> The 2013 Super Bowl champions are the Seattle Seahawks. The Super Bowl champions are (*they* or *them*).
> The Super Bowl Champions are *they*.
> *They* are the Super Bowl Champions.

Try one more:

> The Powerball winner was not (*I* or *me*).
> The Powerball winner was not *I*.
> *I* was not the Powerball winner.

We don't generally follow this rule when we are speaking, but in academic writing, you should.

Who, Whom, Whoever, and Whomever

Another rule we rarely follow in speaking is the distinction among *who, whom, whoever,* and *whomever*. Do you ever hear anyone say *whom*? It's almost unnatural sounding. However, in academic and professional writing, you will want to be able to decide which pronoun to use. If you review Box 8.1, you will see that *who* and *whoever* are subjective pronouns, and *whom* and *whomever* are objective pronouns. You can remember this with the common phrase "To *whom* it may concern" found on so many form letters, where *whom* is the object of the preposition *to*.

A test that can be applied to make the decision between *who* and *whom*, and *whoever* and *whomever* is substituting pronouns that we are more comfortable using. You can substitute *he, she,* or *they* for *who* and *whoever,* and you can substitute *him, her,* or *them* for *whom* and *whomever*. I remember this test by matching *him* and *them* with *whom* because they all end in *m*.

Here are some examples to try this test:

> I enjoy playing volleyball with **whoever/whomever** will play with me.
> I enjoy playing volleyball with **he/him**…

The correct choice is *him* which matches with *whomever*.

> Politicians **who/whom** are always campaigning must think about **who/whom** they represent.
> Politicians **they/them** are always campaigning must think about **he/him** they represent.

The correct choice for the first set is *they* as in *they are always campaigning*, and the correct choice for the second set is *him* as in *must think about him*. Therefore the correct sentence is,

> Politicians *who* are always campaigning must think about *whom* they represent.

When asking a question that starts with Who or Whom, it helps to change the question to a statement.

> *Who* is responsible for mailing the payment? *He* is responsible for mailing the payment. The use of the subjective case *who* is correct.

> *Whom* is Margie falling in love with? Margie is falling in love with *him*. The use of the objective case *whom* is correct.

Courtesy of Margaret Steimer

EXERCISE 8.2

Circle the correct pronoun in the following paragraphs.

My friend Lette and (I / me) love penguins. (We / Us) two are always buying penguin gifts for each

other. Between (she and I / her and me) our favorite penguin is the Emperor Penguin. The largest penguins

are (they / them), standing up to three and a half feet tall. The movie *March of the Penguins* showed (they /

them) in the bitter cold of Antarctica. The female Emperor Penguin is the one (who / whom) hunts for fish,

while the male (he / him) takes care of the egg after breeding season. The males huddle together in a pack to

keep warm, each taking (his / their) turn at being the one in the center of the warm pack.

Penguins might be so popular in our culture because (they / them) do not fear humans. (Their /

There) predators include sharks and orcas. Their black backs and white bellies help camouflage (they / them)

from these predators. When penguins are swimming, (their / there) white bellies blend with the water. (It's

/ Its) reflective surface blends with the white feathers when predators are looking up at (they / them) from

below. People often think a penguin with (its / their) coloring resembles a tuxedo. Although (their / they're)

usually in the water, these flightless birds can waddle on their feet or slide on their bellies. The penguins (who

/ whom) slide on (their / them) bellies are said to be tobogganing.

My friend Lette (who / whom) has the largest penguin collection between the two of (we / us) plans

on traveling to see (they / them) in their natural habitat. Lette, (who / whom) is a well-seasoned traveler,

will not have to travel to Antarctica. (She / Her) will be able to go to the Galapagos Islands off the coast of

Ecuador to see penguins. As for (I / me), it will be delightful to see (she / her) pictures when (she / her)

returns.

Pronouns in Comparisons

Another tricky pronoun rule for writers is the correct pronoun case for comparisons, using the words *than* and *as*. Sometimes in our writing and in our speaking, we leave out words because they are implied. However, different meanings can result from leaving these words out. Consider the following two sentences.

Gina loves her dog more than *I*.

Gina loves her dog more than *me*.

In the first sentence, the assumed message is *Gina loves her dog more than I love her dog.* In the second sentence, the assumed message is *Gina loves her dog more than she loves me.* Careful editing is required for the correct meaning to be conveyed.

When comparisons are made using the words *than* and *as*, it helps to fill in the remaining words to make sure you are using the correct pronoun case.

You are richer than **I/me**. This sentence expanded is, *You are richer than I am rich.* So, the correct choice is *I*.

Your brother is as intelligent as **I/me/mine**. This sentence could be *Your brother is as intelligent as I am intelligent* OR *Your brother is as intelligent as mine.* It all depends on the writer's meaning.

-self Pronouns

Another type of pronoun that we use in the English language is the *–self* pronoun. This pronoun has the ending of *–self* or *-selves*. Box 8.3 illustrates the *–self* pronouns.

BOX 8.3

-self Pronouns	
myself	ourselves
yourself	yourselves
himself, herself, itself	themselves

NOTE: The following constructions are not words: hisself, theirself, and theirselves.

These pronouns can be used in sentences only if they rename a subject or another noun in the sentence.

The opera singer could not dress *herself* in the elaborate costume. (*Herself* refers back to the subject *singer*.)

I will have to rely on *myself* to find the country road since my GPS is not working. (*Myself* refers back to the subject *I*.)

People cannot depend on money *itself* to control their happiness. (*Itself* refers back to the object *money*.)

You should not use the–*self* pronouns when personal pronouns in the subjective or objective case should be used.

> NO: My friends and myself will go to Florida for spring break.
>
> YES: My friends and I will go to Florida for spring break.
>
> NO: You can leave the decision making to themselves.
>
> YES: You can leave the decision making to them.

Relative Pronouns

Relative pronouns include *who, whom, whose, which,* and *that.* These pronouns refer to a noun and provide more information about that noun.

> Mary, *who* is older than her brother, will be entering the Peace Corps in January.

NOTE: It is important to remember that *who, whom,* and *whose* are used with people; *which* and *that* refer to animals and things.

> NO: Athletes that want to get ahead should work out everyday.
>
> YES: Athletes who want to get ahead should work out everyday.

Pronoun Reference

The noun that the pronoun is standing in for is called an **antecedent**. Pronouns must refer to their antecedent precisely. Because pronouns are such great "short cuts" for writers, often a problem occurs in writing when there is no clear antecedent for a pronoun. Writers can avoid this problem by keeping pronouns close to their antecedents and by making sure all pronouns have precise antecedents.

Unclear Pronoun References

If one pronoun could stand for more than one antecedent, you are better off using a noun than a pronoun. For example, consider the following sentence:

> I shoved the sweater into the drawer even though *it* was dirty.

The closest noun that the pronoun *it* can refer to is *drawer.* A reader will wonder what is dirty, the sweater or the drawer? Careful writers will revise the sentence to be clearer:

> I shoved the sweater into the drawer even though the sweater was dirty.

Here is another example of an unclear pronoun reference:

> Andrew told his uncle that *he* had no money.

A reader will wonder who has no money, Andrew or his uncle? The sentence can be revised to be clearer:

> Andrew had no money, and he told his uncle.

Sometimes the antecedent is missing entirely. This omission happens frequently when writers use the pronouns *it, that, this, they,* and *which.*

> We told our friends that we were getting married, *which* made our parents quite happy.

Are the parents happy because we told our friends or because we were getting married? A clearer pronoun reference is made with one of the following sentences.

> Our parents were quite happy because we told our friends about our impending marriage.
>
> Our parents were quite happy because we were getting married.

Often a sentence that starts with *it, that,* or *this* will lack clear pronoun reference.

> I couldn't find a new outfit nor quite lose 20 more pounds in time for my reunion. *This* further upset me.

A reader will wonder what is upsetting, not finding a new outfit, not losing 20 more pounds, or both? Usually a writer will want to use a noun to make the meaning clearer.

> I couldn't find a new outfit nor quite lose 20 more pounds in time for my reunion. *These challenges* further upset me.

EXERCISE 8.3

Revise the following sentences to make clear pronoun references. You might have to add nouns and other wording to make the pronoun references clear.

1. Paul plays the bass drum very well, but he keeps it hidden.

2. The writer has written a biography of John Steinbeck that reveals his unusual philosophy.

3. Andy's secret dream is to be a gourmet chef, but he has never tried it.

4. When Beth's parents finally got her to the emergency room, they put her leg in a cast.

5. When we entered the football stadium, they were already ahead by twenty-one points.

6. Many companies dislike their employees dating because they see it as having fun on their time.

7. Although Jackson cried for ten minutes after scraping his elbow, finally it ended.

8. When Cindy put the wineglass on the glass-topped table, it broke.

9. After Brian left our house, John found his car keys.

10. Researchers are studying what makes people depressed; they know good health and close relationships are extremely important.

Using *You*

I use *you* in this textbook to refer to you, my reader. However, careful writers only use *you* to mean the readers directly. Only use the second-person pronoun *you* when you mean **all** of your readers. Do not use *you* to mean *people*.

> NO: Poker moves like these can help or hurt you in a game of poker.
> YES: Poker moves like these can help or hurt a player in a game of poker.
> NO: As an aircraft controller, you have to be alert at all times.
> YES: An aircraft controller has to be alert at all times.
> NO: In Saudi Arabia, you usually have no waiting times at gas pumps.
> YES: In Saudi Arabia, drivers usually have no waiting times at gas pumps.

Many problems exist with using the second-person point-of-view or "you" view:

> Some instructors believe that the second-person point-of-view has no role in formal academic writing.
> Writers have to be confident that when they use "you" in their writing, they are referring to all readers. Sometimes a piece of writing will have multiple readers from various backgrounds.
> Writers who use the second-person point-of-view risk distancing their readers if the readers do not feel like "you" applies to them.

EXERCISE 8.4

Read the following paragraphs that were written for a general audience, including college students. Then answer the questions following this passage.

When you first try heroin, your last thought is that you'll get addicted. But chances are you will. According to the National Institute on Drug Abuse, 4.2 million Americans who are twelve years of age or older have used heroin at least once in 2011. It is estimated that 23 percent become dependent on it. The problem is that you just feel so good on "H." It makes you feel so confident and settled. Pretty soon you will do anything to score. You're like a wild animal hunting for your drug. You crave the drug so badly that you know you just have to have it, or you won't be able to get out of bed in the morning. If you don't have your drug, you feel all of this anxiety, and you feel like you have bugs running through your skin.

Eventually, your habit will cause you to run out of money. You resort to stealing from your friends and family, so you can feed your addiction. In time, you find yourself having ruined every relationship in your life. You know you have to get clean, but your options are limited. Methadone can help you because it works on your brain in the same way as heroin, only slower. You can only get "meth" from an outpatient treatment program, and you have to go there on a daily basis. Generally, you're more likely to end up in jail as a result of your addiction, instead of being able to beat the drug.

1. What is the effect of the writer using second-person point-of-view or "you"?

2. How can the writer revise the point-of-view for this piece of writing?

EXERCISE 8.5

Revise the following sentences to eliminate the second-person "you" point-of-view. Make the revisions consistent with third-person point-of-view. As you revise, imagine that you are writing to a general audience that includes people of all ages and backgrounds.

1. Facebook is a website in which you can document your life.

2. You are able to share statuses, pictures, and videos from your experiences.

3. During college registration, you discuss your next semester courses with your advisor.

4. In college, you don't get your final grades until the end of the semester.

5. Fathers may not know what kinds of clothing or toys their children like, but they know what problems you have.

6. Happy marriages happen when you can still be independent, yet you know someone has your back.

7. When you are in a foreign country, you should be respectful to your "host" country and follow its customs.

8. While you are visiting India, you might find yourself thinking that you're in a prior century.

9. If you are arrested, you are allowed to make a phone call.

10. Your time in a jail cell is not a time that you will likely forget.

CHAPTER 9
Belief

© 2014 somchaij. Used under license from Shutterstock, Inc.

PERSUASION—TAKING A POSITION

Chances are you are quite used to writing position papers that are sometimes also called reaction papers or response papers. Reaction papers require that you respond to something you read or a film that you watch, and then you add your experiences to shape an assertive claim. These papers move beyond a summary. A summary is more like a book report that you probably wrote in elementary school. When you take a position or react to something, you are moving beyond reporting what you read or saw. You are persuading your readers that your reaction is valid or true.

Another stimulus for a position paper is an issue. We are surrounded by so many events, problems, and issues every day. It is human nature to take a position on many of these issues. You have plenty to say about so many issues that matter to you. Two important ideas behind taking a position and presenting it persuasively are providing reasons for your position and making sure those reasons are well-grounded. Your personal experiences and values are generally what form those reasons.

So far, much of this book has been about writing to explain. When you are writing to explain, you include a certain amount of persuasion too. You want your reader to be persuaded that you know what you are writing about and you know that it is important. When you write a position paper, you are explaining as well, but you are also making a claim to create an effect in your reader's mind. You want your readers to consider your ideas and possibly be moved to think differently than they had been thinking before reading your writing.

Persuasion is also referred to as argument. The two terms are used interchangeably. Argument has an unfortunate connotation of debating, or worse yet, fighting. For this purpose, I prefer to use the term persuasion, but you should know that your experience with argumentative writing is the same as persuasive writing. As a writer, you are providing a reasonable position and defending this position with plenty of reasons and evidence.

We have covered many methods of development in this book: narrating, describing, illustrating, analyzing, evaluating, comparing, and contrasting. You are able to have all of these methods available to you when you write persuasively. Furthermore, when you write a position paper often you are agreeing and disagreeing about others' ideas. You now have the opportunity to consider viewpoints different than your own, and you can sometimes demonstrate the limits or shortfalls of these viewpoints. You can also create your own position that covers these shortfalls.

At the same time, you can use others' ideas to support your own ideas. Ideas that are similar to your own, help to support or bolster your position. Support in persuasive writing is extremely important. Your reasons and examples should be logical and fair.

Ethos, Pathos, and Logos

If those three terms are unfamiliar to you, do not worry. They have a deep history, going back to the Greeks' oral debating in Socrates' time, approximately 400 BC. The use of ethos, pathos, and logos helps you in persuasive writing because it allows you to think about issues in a fair and logical way.

When writers use ethos, they are appealing to the reader's sense of ethics and values. Readers will only be persuaded if they feel the writer is fair and credible. Readers are eager to read new and interesting ideas, but in order for them to believe you, they must first believe in your fairness. You can achieve this by using qualifying terms in your writing (refer to Box 6.1 in Chapter 6) and by giving careful consideration to others' viewpoints.

Additionally, using sources that agree with you or that provide information that you did not know before you encountered it also helps your ethos. If you are not an authority about something, it helps to include an authority. However, you should certainly only use sources if your assignment permits it, and only use sources that are credible and reliable. If you use a source that is unreliable, then your reader will find your ethos suffering and will find your writing unreliable.

When writers use pathos, they are appealing to the reader's emotions. Have you ever read something that made you laugh out loud or cry? That writer achieved pathos. You can affect your reader's emotions by using expressive and descriptive language. Also, narration or telling a story often creates pathos. When readers' emotions are affected, they tend to be more easily persuaded. Having pathos in your writing has to be well-tempered, however. You do not want to overdo it with emotional appeals especially in certain kinds of academic writing, although it is useful depending on the writing situation. And being aware of pathos is paramount in understanding and evaluating others' persuasive writing, which you will encounter your entire life.

Logos is the most prevalent appeal in academic writing. This is the logical reasoning behind a writer's argument. When writers use logos, they provide research and data to appeal to their reader's sense of reasoning. It is human nature to be persuaded when confronted with data, research, and statistics. Writers have to be careful with their use of logos, however. You do not want to make false claims because you did not carefully review data. You also do not want to supply data that only you think is true or that you invented simply to sound more reasonable.

Table 9.1 provides you with the definition of ethos, pathos, and logos, and it gives you some examples from visuals, like print advertising, and text.

TABLE 9.1	Persuasive Appeals in Visual and Textual Literacy		
	Definition	**Visual**	**Textual**
Ethos	Ethical Appeal to audience through fairness, authority, and credibility of author	Trademarks, symbols, icons, signs, use of celebrities	Rapport with reader; use of qualifying terms like "might" and "perhaps"; consideration of alternative viewpoints; using authorities other than the author
Pathos	Emotional Appeal to audience	Appeal to senses (for example, taste); appeal to human qualities: humor, compassion, sex appeal	Connection to values and beliefs; expressive language; narratives
Logos	Logical Appeal to audience	Statistics, research, data, details	Statistics, research, data; structured argument with evidence and reasoning

One way to think about persuasion is through the ultimate persuasion, advertising. We are constantly confronted with advertisements. And we are doing the advertising ourselves when we wear certain clothing, for instance, a baseball hat with a Nike® swoosh. Our television shows now insert advertising into them by having the characters eat a certain brand of cereal, for example. Advertising uses ethos, pathos, and logos in order to entice consumers into purchasing products.

Prompt 9.1

Find three advertisements from magazines or newspapers that you feel are effective. Using Table 9.1 for help, explain how ethos, pathos, and logos are used in each of the advertisements. Write one paragraph for each advertisement. Your professor might want you to bring these advertisements to class, so be prepared to print them out if you found them on a computer.

Response Paper—A Student Example

Last semester, my first-year writing students watched the documentary *Bully*, which was originally titled *The Bully Project*. This documentary was directed by Lee Hirsch and filmed in the 2009–2010 school year. The film crew followed five public school students and their families as they faced bullying everyday. The documentary was far-reaching in its effects from educating the public about bullying to creating a call to action to put a stop to bullying in schools.

My students were assigned a response paper to the documentary. They were asked to avoid summarizing the documentary, and, instead, to use their own personal experiences and the experiences of those they know to write a short essay. Their audience was a wide one—current college students, professors, and parents.

The assignment was embraced by my students. It seems everyone has something to say about bullying. The documentary further created outrage and reminded my students about their own personal experiences. What follows is one student's response paper. I have renamed the student writer Jonathan Black.

Jonathan Black
Dr. Shipley
Essay #1
October 22, 2013

Bullying the Little Guy

After watching the documentary *Bully*, I thought just how unfair these five kids had it with being bullied because of their appearance, their disabilities, or their sexual orientation. It seems kids are bullied if they show the slightest difference from what is perceived as "normal." Some kids who are bullied see no way out from the bullying, and they ultimately end their own lives, as was shown in the film. As for the bullies themselves, they seem to think hitting kids or picking on kids smaller than they are is harmless fun. Bullying sometimes can be met with retaliation, where the kid who is being bullied defends himself successfully.

When I was in high school, there was this one kid Jason whom everyone seemed to mess with. I became friends with him because I didn't like seeing him being pushed around by bullies who were bigger than he was. When the bullies saw that I became friends with Jason, they seemed to only bother him when he was by himself. Jason would always tell me when one of the kids pushed him into a locker or held his throat with a chokehold. I approached the bullies one day and asked them why they continued to bully Jason. They told me they did it because it is fun and school is so boring that they needed something to do. This information further angered me, and I decided to take matters into my own hands.

One day I told Jason to meet me after school, so I could teach him how to defend himself. I took him to a nearby boxing gym where I practiced for my own boxing tournaments. The look on Jason's face when he saw the boxing gym was like he had just won a million dollars. He trained with me for two weeks. After the two weeks of training, I told Jason that he was prepared to handle himself if the bullies started messing with him. I also made him promise me that he wouldn't just walk up to the bullies and start fighting them. He promised me that he wouldn't, but that promise didn't last very long.

One day before school, I met Jason, so I could be with him if the bullies tried anything. We walked into school, and the bullies were standing outside of the cafeteria. Jason looked at me, smiled, and ran up to one of the bullies and swung blows to his face repeatedly. I pulled Jason off of the bully and ran him to the bathroom to talk to him. I asked him what happened to his promise, and he said that he couldn't help himself. He said, "When I saw him, I just snapped and took all of my anger out." I couldn't get mad at him because I knew where he was coming from. When we left the bathroom, Jason was called to the office and was suspended from school for a week. When he returned to school, no one thought about bullying him again.

I'm not sure if what we did was right, but I know I felt good about it. In the documentary *Bully*, no one seemed to care about the kids who were being bullied except their families. The teachers and other adults seemed helpless like they didn't know what to do or didn't think it was that big of a deal. Bullying needs to stop, and if it comes down to giving the bullies what they deserve, then at least the problem is solved.

© 2014 sirastock. Used under license from Shutterstock, Inc.

Reaction to Writing

1. I often use the concept of a springboard with my students to explain to them that what they are responding to should be a starting point into their own ideas for writing. How does Jonathan use the documentary as a springboard for his response paper?

2. Underline Jonathan's thesis statement. How does he use his personal experience to support his thesis statement?

3. In your opinion, does Jonathan's personal experience provide enough support for his thesis statement? Why or why not?

Finding a Topic

You will write position papers and response papers in many of your college courses, not just your writing and English courses. You will write persuasively to defend your position, when you are asked whether you agree or disagree with _____. Or you will be expected to write a position paper to state that _____ is fair or unfair, true or false, or good or bad.

If you're fortunate enough to select your own topic, you should find a specific topic that is narrow enough for you to cover successfully with the length requirement given. You should also have some knowledge and experience with the topic especially if you are not using sources. And most importantly, you should care deeply about the topic. Persuasive writing has a good deal of energy and zest to it. If you aren't feeling this zest, your writing will show it. And if you were able to select your own topic, your reader will wonder why you selected the one that you did when your writing ends up being dull and lifeless.

Opinions

One source of endless issues that you can easily comb through is a newspaper. Whether online or in print, local or national, a newspaper is full of issues that you can address in a position paper. There is one particular section of a newspaper that looks at debatable issues—the opinion section, sometimes called the editorial section, or op/ed for short.

"Watch What You Say on OC's Boardwalk"

The following editorial is about the issue of whether to post signs that discourage swearing on the boardwalk of Ocean City, Maryland, an Atlantic Ocean coastal town. Virginia Beach, Virginia, put up signs over ten years ago that say "No Swearing." Additionally, in Virginia Beach, if you are caught swearing and it leads to a "breach of the peace," you are subjected to a third-degree misdemeanor punishable by a fine of up to $500. This editorial first appeared in the *Ocean Pines Independent* on February 5, 2014. As you read the editorial, consider the following question:

○ What's at issue?

WATCH WHAT YOU SAY ON OC'S BOARDWALK

@!&#% it, Ocean City, we know you are trying to be a family-friendly resort and protect your tourism industry, but sometimes it's just so *@!&#% hard to do, what with free-speech rights and all.   1

While the urge to impose bans and make new laws is sometimes compelling, as officials at Maryland's seaside resort acknowledge, this is not always the best path to correcting a societal problem. This is especially true when the problem is more nuisance than direct threat to anyone's health or safety.   2

Imminent threats like driving while impaired or criminal assaults clearly require laws and enforcement to keep us safe. But public profanity is one of those areas where one man's trash is another man's treasure, so to speak. And then, just when you think you've got it right, legally speaking, bam—you get slapped with a lawsuit over freedom of speech.   3

Ocean City officials are on the right track, though, by pursuing a better means to curb public profanity on its iconic Boardwalk. Following Virginia Beach's lead and utilizing what can be a more powerful force than the long arm of the law, OC officials are looking at a public awareness campaign that asks people not to swear on the Boardwalk. Posting signs to that effect will give those people who are strolling the Boards something to point to and say, "Hey, did you see the sign? Please stop," or something to that effect.   4

People should be encouraged to speak if they are offended or don't like what they hear. Peer pressure is powerful force, as the tobacco industry is finding out. Thirty years ago, if bans on public smoking had been proposed anywhere at all in this country, they would have been met with fierce resistance by an adult populace that almost universally smoked incessantly.   5

Today, anyone who lights up anywhere in public meets with immediate dirty looks and disparaging remarks. People feel empowered to speak up.   6

In the beginning, many (perhaps most) folks may feel uncomfortable asking a stranger to stop swearing. That's why Boardwalk merchants should support the cause. And resort police should maintain a visible presence, just in case a verbal request escalates.   7

When it becomes clear that public profanity is as reviled and unwelcome as smoking in public, those who are in the habit of using such language will either go elsewhere or change their habits. If a scuffle ensues or threats are made, other laws—like disorderly conduct—will empower police to intervene swiftly.   8

Consistent peer pressure and appeals for courtesy and civility are, in the end, the best weapons for fighting this battle.   9

Reaction to Writing

1. If you do not know the meanings of the following words, try to determine their meaning from the surrounding context in the editorial. Check their meanings in a dictionary and write a sentence using each word.

    imminent (3)

    iconic (4)

    populace (5)

    incessantly (5)

    disparaging (6)

    reviled (8)

    scuffle (8)

    intervene (8)

2. The symbols @!&#% are used to show swearing in text and is often called grawlix. Where else have you seen grawlix? What is the effect of using grawlix twice in the first paragraph?

3. How effective is the comparison between the ban on public smoking and a potential ban on public profanity? Why?

Prompt 9.2

At the beginning of this editorial, you were asked to consider, "What's at issue?" First, answer this question as a form of brainstorming to consider **all** parts of this issue. Then write a double-spaced, one to two paged letter to the editor responding to the issue of public profanity. Spend some time preparing your ideas about how Ocean City can curb swearing on its boardwalk, or even if it should. Begin your letter with "Dear Editor," and end it with a closing like "Sincerely," and your name.

Making Claims

When we write persuasively, we make claims or assertions, and these claims generally become our thesis statements. A common way to make a claim for a position paper is to use the words "should" or "should not." A fairly simple way to think about this is with the following formula:

topic or issue + should or should not + your position = your thesis statement

With more and more college courses having online formats or a combination of traditional classroom time and an online format, we'll work with the following example:

College courses should/should not require attendance.

Collecting Evidence

You have to do some deep thinking when you write persuasively. You want to make sure you have all the necessary support, and you want to look at the issue from all angles. Remember that generally no issue is simply black and white. Complex issues operate in the murky grey area, and that is where you should operate, as well, in writing for college. You want to question the assumptions that you have in regards to an issue, and you will need to question the assumptions others have too.

When you write persuasively, you have two goals:

1. You need to defend your position with your own **good** evidence.
2. You need to consider all other positions in regards to your issue.

When you are first developing your ideas, you shouldn't be too quick to choose a side of an issue. You should have an open mind to all possibilities. You want to have the best reasons for your position in your essay. The only way to find the best reasons is to uncover all the reasons.

EXERCISE 9.1

Working individually or with a partner, brainstorm to find **all** of the reasons for both of the following working thesis statements:

College courses should require attendance because . . .

College courses should not require attendance because . . .

Testing and Organizing Your Evidence

You probably gathered many reasons when you completed Exercise 9.1. If you didn't get the opportunity, you will want to discuss these reasons with someone else. Now that you have so many reasons, you will want to separate the good from the bad. There is little sense in worrying about reasons that your readers will find trivial or ridiculous. Once you have looked at all the reasons for both sides of the issue, you should have a sense about what your position is and what those who disagree with you think.

You also might have to do some qualifying to avoid making generalizations. For instance, did you find that even the term "college courses" is too broad? Maybe you think classroom attendance should be required for certain courses. Did you find the term "attendance" a bit abstract or hazy? What constitutes attendance? This type of deep thinking will also have you challenging your assumptions.

As you sort through your evidence, you want to find the evidence that rises to the top as being the best and the evidence that is relevant to your essay. You will want to find this for both sides of the issue because you will need to include the opposing viewpoint in your essay. When you include the opposing viewpoint, you will be able to use your evidence to overcome this opposing viewpoint.

Before you draft your essay, it will be helpful to organize your reasons or your evidence. Persuasive writing often is organized in order of importance with your best reason last. How you include your other evidence should be structured according to how you can move easily and naturally from one point to the next. Where you put the opposing viewpoint is a matter of how likely your readers will be to agree with you. If your sense is that your audience will be hostile to your ideas, you will do better trying to overcome their objections early in your essay. Remember that rarely can you turn readers' opinions around 180 degrees, but if you can create just a flicker of consideration for your ideas, you have done well.

Prompt 9.3

Continue your work from Exercise 9.1 and write a double-spaced, two paged position paper using the skills covered in this chapter. Consider revising the working thesis statement to suit your position and your reasons. Be sure to have your thesis statement as the last sentence of your introduction. Your intended audience is your professors and classmates.

Prompt 9.4

Using the skills covered in this chapter, write a double-spaced, two to three paged position paper about an illegal or dangerous behavior typical of teenagers or young adults. Include your position on how authorities should respond to it. How harshly should such behavior be punished, if at all? Provide your own original reasons to support your position. Some ideas to consider, although you are not limited to these, are the following:

Bullying or Cyber bullying

Reckless driving

Downloading music without paying for it

The latest drug or alcohol trend

You will need to narrow the issue you choose considerably for the length of this assignment. Your intended audience is readers of your college newspaper. Be sure to have your thesis statement as the last sentence of your introduction. Make sure you consider all the evidence for all angles of the issue. You will also want to include the opposing viewpoints of those who would disagree with you.

SHIFTING SENTENCES AND PARAGRAPHS

Now that your memory has been refreshed in regards to verb tense and pronoun agreement, you are ready to take on another important concept in sentence structure, unintentional shifts. A shift is an unnecessary change in person (point-of-view), number, and verb tense. Your readers expect you to stay in, for example, one verb tense within one sentence and not to shift abruptly to another verb tense within the same sentence.

A. Avoid shifting point-of-view or person. The point-of-view for writing is the perspective from which it is written: first-person (I or we), second-person (you), or third-person (he, she, it, they, or any noun).

   NO: Our class practiced singing the National Anthem for the season opener of our football team. We learned how to get to the high notes or at least pretend to reach them. *You* were embarrassed by the professor if *you* did not have the words memorized.

   YES: Our class practiced singing the National Anthem for the season opener of our football team. We learned how to get to the high notes or at least pretend to reach them. *We* were embarrassed by the professor if *we* did not have the words memorized.

Be especially alert to writing sentences that are like commands. You do not want to shift from third-person point-of-view to a command sentence which is second-person point-of-view, implied.

   NO: Drivers should be careful in my neighborhood. Slow down and watch for deer.

   YES: Drivers should be careful in my neighborhood. They need to slow down and watch for deer.

B. Avoid shifting in number from singular to plural or plural to singular. You learned this in Chapter 7 in the pronoun agreement section.

   NO: When an employee is treated with respect, they are more motivated to do a good job. (*Employee* is singular, and the pronoun *they* is plural.)

You have four different ways to fix this shift.

   1. The most effective approach is to cast the sentence to all plural. Make sure everything is changed to plural.

   YES: When *employees are* treated with respect, they are more motivated to do good *jobs*.

   2. Sometimes you can eliminate the pronoun altogether.

   YES: An employee who is treated with respect is more motivated to do a good job.

   3. Sometimes you can use an article (a, an, the) instead of the pronoun.

   4. The least effective way to fix the shift is to use the wordy expressions *him or her*, *he or she*, and *his or her*.

   YES: When an employee is treated with respect, *he or she is* more motivated to do a good job.

C. Avoid shifting from one verb tense to another when the time of the action is the same.

   NO: There was no way I could stay with my girlfriend after she cheated on me. Just as I was going to break up with her, a friend *calls* me to tell me it *is* all a joke. (The verb tense shifts from past tense to present tense.)

   YES: There was no way I could stay with my girlfriend after she cheated on me. Just as I was going to break up with her, a friend *called* me to tell me it *was* all a joke.

D. Avoid shifts between indirect dialogue and direct dialogue. Indirect dialogue is reporting what someone said. The word *that* is often used for indirect dialogue.

INDIRECT: My mother said that if I didn't get home soon all the lasagna would be gone.

Direct dialogue uses quotation marks. It is actually quoting what someone said.

DIRECT: My mother said, "If you don't get home soon all the lasagna will be gone."

NOTE: Commas and periods go inside quotation marks.

NO: The base runner said he thought he had been safe at third base and please review the tape.

YES: The base runner said he thought he had been safe at third base and asked to have the play reviewed. (The sentence is cast in all indirect dialogue.)

YES: The base runner said, "I was safe at third base. Please review the tape." (The sentence is cast in all direct dialogue.)

EXERCISE 9.2

Revise the following sentences to correct the shifts in person, number, and verb tense, and shifts between indirect and direct dialogue.

1. Going to a fraternity party will not help anyone score an A on their test, so studying would be the best thing to do first.

2. In order to be punctual, students must keep track of everything they have to do. Buy a planner and use it every day. Write down all assignment and appointments in it.

3. The professor asked did we enjoy the documentary?

4. The biggest problem every freshman has during their first semester of college is a lack of time management skills.

5. A first-year seminar series started at the college in 2005 as administrators try to support first-year students as much as they can.

6. If students need help with their schoolwork or advice about personal matters, don't be afraid to ask for it.

7. One way for a student to keep motivated is thinking about how proud your family is that you are going to college.

8. Being in a quiet place to study helps students relax and concentrate on the work he or she is doing.

9. The parents worried about making ends meet with triplets in college. For years, they live on a tight budget to save.

10. When students need a break, he or she suggests, "Let's go shoot some hoops."

WRITING CONCLUSIONS TO ESSAYS

A good conclusion is like a good night kiss at the end of a spectacular date. You want it to linger on your date's lips long after you went your separate ways. And, like that magical good night kiss, the conclusion to an essay makes your reader desiring more.

Readers should continue thinking about your essay's ideas long after they stop reading. Creating a memorable conclusion can be a tough job, but, fortunately, writers have many options:

○ Look back at your introduction. If you started your essay by telling a story, you could return to that same story. This method is like a "bookend" approach. Your essay stands upright with two bookends, the introduction and the conclusion, on either side of it.

○ Challenge your reader to doing something with this information. This "call to action" approach is especially effective in persuasive writing.

○ Connect your ideas to what is still needed to be known. Your reader will want to continue finding out more about your ideas and other ideas connected to them.

○ Emphasize how your considerably narrow topic is just a small slice of a huge pie. For example, if you wrote a position paper about why *Brave New World* should be read in public high schools despite some parents' disapproval about the sexual and drug-related references, you can end by showing your readers how censorship waters down curriculum and limits students from engaging in controversial issues.

○ Consider having one more example or image that connects to your thesis. Although you probably have been told "no new ideas" in conclusions, having a memorable detail or example that connects to your ideas is certainly a good possibility.

○ Most conclusions can be rather short. If you are finding yourself with a long, drawn-out conclusion, try deleting the last few sentences to find a crisper ending.

○ Pay attention to the style of your conclusion, especially the last sentence. If you have a nice rhythm or balance in your sentence structure, your reader will be left with a good sound of finality.

○ Conclusions should end on a positive note.

Some things you want to avoid in writing your conclusion include the following:

○ Avoid repeating your thesis statement or any of your reasons and examples when your essay is rather short, less than ten pages. Too many student writers have been told to "restate" their thesis statement in the conclusion. This does not mean "repeat" your thesis statement.

○ Short essays, shorter than ten pages, do not need summaries in the conclusion. Summing up your ideas for a short essay insults your reader's memory.

○ As I wrote above, you can end with new examples or new reasons that connect to your thesis statement; however, you should not bring in new ideas that will disrupt the unity of your essay.

○ If you are using sources, do not bring in a new source in the conclusion. And, always end with your own words and ideas, not a source's.

○ Avoid apologizing for anything in the essay. I'm not sure why some writers do this in the conclusion or anywhere in the essay, for that matter, but I have seen it too many times, and it is weak and ineffectual.

○ Never end with "in conclusion," "to conclude," "in summary," or any other phrases like these. Your readers know the end is near; don't insult their intelligence.

GUIDANCE FOR WRITING ASSIGNMENTS

You will be assigned writing in many of your college courses, not just your English and writing courses. You could even have a written assignment in a math class. Because you will be writing in many different subject areas, for many different professors, you should always make sure that you understand the writing assignments thoroughly. Some professors will not give you much guidance when they assign an essay or a research paper. This does not mean you can't seek out more guidance from the professor. Don't be afraid to ask questions so that you understand a writing assignment completely.

NOTE: When in doubt, always assume that everything you write in college requires formal academic prose.

The following list contains questions you can ask your professor when you are given a writing assignment.

○ Should I turn in my first draft?
○ Can I make an appointment to go over my first draft with you?
○ Can I revise and resubmit my paper once it is graded?
○ Is there a length requirement? If so, is it by the number of pages, paragraphs, or words?
○ Should I include a cover page? Should the paper be placed in a binder or a folder?
○ Can I submit my paper via e-mail? If so, is it due at the beginning of class or at any time on the due date?
○ Are late papers accepted? If so, what is the penalty?

○ Do I need to use outside sources? How many?

○ Can I use online sources?

○ Do I need to provide copies of my sources?

○ Can the class textbook be used as a source?

○ What documentation style should be used? MLA? APA? Chicago?

○ Can I use contractions?

○ Can I use the first-person point-of-view *I*?

○ Can I use anecdotal evidence?

○ Can I use my own personal experience?

COMMAS

Commas are so important for readers. Readers of the English language see a comma, and it signals to them to expect a change in the sentence structure. You might have been taught to insert commas in places where you pause while reading. This is only partly true. Writers use commas in many places to allow the reader to pause **and** to help the reader understand the sentence.

Let's consider all the comma rules that you already know.

1. Use a comma after one independent clause that is connected to another independent clause with one of the FANBOYS (for, and, nor, but, or, yet, so). This is called a compound sentence. Take note that the comma goes **before** the conjunction.

   Frozen is the highest-earning Disney movie ever, and its song "Let it Go" is equally successful.

2. Use a comma after a dependent clause that is followed by an independent clause.

   Because Bruno Mars was coming to my hometown for a summer concert, I waited in line all night to get tickets.

   When a dependent clause follows an independent clause, a comma is not needed unless a contrast is being made, or the dependent clause is an afterthought.

   Classes were cancelled for the remainder of the week because it snowed.

   Classes were cancelled for the remainder of the week, although they will have to be made up online. (A contrast is being made with *although*.)

   We will postpone the upcoming meeting to later in November, if that is suitable to you. (The dependent clause is an afterthought.)

3. To show a relationship between two complete sentences a semicolon can be used with a transitional expression. When a transitional expression is used after the semicolon, it must be followed with a comma.

   Tim will be graduating college this May; therefore, he needs to start his job search.

Comma rules sometimes seem like they vary from one teacher to the next. In academic writing, however, it is better to err on the side of caution and use all of the necessary commas. In different writing formats, comma rules are much more flexible. For example, in journalism, commas are often not used in the places you would use them in academic writing. This is due to space constraints. Additionally, computer software programs like grammar check are quite weak when it comes to helping writers insert commas. For this reason, writers need to know comma rules to help readers understand their sentences. What follows, then, are additional rules for using commas in academic writing.

4. Use a comma after an introductory word and an introductory phrase that starts the sentence. A phrase is a group of related words that is missing both a subject and a verb. This use of the comma allows the reader to know where the main sentence begins.

   Yes, I will go see Bonnie at the hospital this evening.

   After dinner, I will go see Bonnie in the hospital.

5. Use a comma to separate three or more elements (words, phrases, or short clauses) in a series. This rule is often referred to as the "serial comma." Careful writers will make sure the final comma before the conjunction, usually *and*, is used.

   The simple dinner consisted of soup, salad, and bread. (This series has three words.)

   The job requires the employee to answer phones politely, pay bills in a timely manner, inspect properties periodically, and attend monthly board meetings. (This series has four phrases.)

   Seniors will register the first week of February, juniors will register the second week of February, sophomores will register the third week of February, and freshmen will register the last week of February. (This series has four short independent clauses.)

6. A thoughtful writer uses transitional words and expressions to help the reader follow along with the writer's thoughts. Box 9.1 lists some commonly used transitional words and expressions.

BOX 9.1

Transitional Words and Expressions		
all things considered	however	needless to say
as a matter of fact	in addition	nevertheless
as a result	incidentally	no doubt
as a rule	in fact	of course
at the same time	in my opinion	on the contrary
consequently	in the first place	on the other hand
for example	in the meantime	therefore
furthermore	moreover	under the circumstances

When a transitional expression could be removed from a sentence without changing its meaning, then it should be set off with commas. In other words, the transitional expression is nonessential. If the transitional expression is needed to understand the sentence and thus can not be removed from the sentence, then no commas are used. This kind of transitional expression is essential.

> I will, in the meantime, take a hot bath while we wait for his news. (The expression *in the meantime* can be removed without changing the meaning of the sentence.)

> I have no doubt that I will stay awake until I hear his news. (The expression *no doubt* is needed to understand the sentence.)

7. A word or words that come immediately before or after a noun or a pronoun and rename the noun or pronoun are called appositives. When an appositive could be removed from the sentence without changing its meaning, then it should be set off with commas. The appositive is nonessential. When an appositive is necessary to the meaning of the sentence, then it is essential and does not require commas.

Consider which of the two sentences is punctuated correctly with commas.

> My mother, Fay, is an excellent cook.

> My mother Fay is an excellent cook.

If you selected the first one, you are correct. I have only one mother, so her name is simply added information and is not essential to the meaning of the sentence. As a writer, you have to know how you punctuate a sentence, so your meaning is received by the reader as you intended.

Consider the following two sentences:

> My brother, J.C., lives in Pennsylvania.

> My brother J.C. lives in Pennsylvania.

Which sentence tells the reader that I have more than one brother?

If you chose the second one, you are correct. However, I have only one brother, so I would write the first sentence. Since I have only one brother, his name is just added information that is not necessary for my intended meaning.

8. When a dependent clause could be removed without changing the meaning of the sentence, then it should be set off with commas. The clause is nonessential. When a dependent clause is necessary or essential to the meaning of the sentence then no commas are used.

Our local grocery store, which is next to my drycleaner, is now going to remain open twenty-four hours a day. (The clause which is next to my drycleaner is nonessential to the meaning of the sentence. It is simply added information; therefore, commas should be inserted.)

People who buy cigarettes for teenagers are breaking the law. (The clause *who buy cigarettes for teenagers* is essential, thus commas should not be inserted.)

9. Use a comma to separate two or more adjectives that describe a noun in equal ways. An easy way to think about this rule is to think of the comma as standing in for the missing word *and*. If you can insert *and* instead of the comma, and it makes sense, then commas should be used.

   The sincere young man could not stop apologizing to me. (It would not make sense to say "the sincere *and* young man," so no commas should be used.)

   The ripe, juicy summer tomato was one of the best I have ever had. (It would make sense to say "the ripe *and* juicy summer tomato," so a comma should be used.)

   NOTE: No comma should be used between the final adjective and the noun after it.

   NO: The ripe, juicy, summer tomato was one of the best I have ever had.

10. Verbs in the *–ing* form are often modifying phrases, and these phrases should be close to the noun or pronoun that they are modifying. They also have commas surrounding them.

    The cat, climbing swiftly up the tree, escaped from the raccoon that was chasing it.

Additional Comma Rules

You probably are aware of many of the comma rules that follow, but it should be helpful to be reminded of a few of them.

11. When you directly address someone by name, commas should surround the name.

    Having your wedding at the Yacht Club is an excellent idea, Erika.

    Fortunately, Jim, you can have the last of the blueberry pie.

    This rule applies to one of my favorite t-shirts that has the following two sentences imprinted on it, followed by "Punctuation Saves Lives." Do you see the important role of the one comma?

    Let's eat Grandma.

    Let's eat, Grandma.

12. Dates having more than two parts require commas for each additional part.

    The meeting was held October 15 in the penthouse of the apartment building. (No comma is needed for a date with two parts.)

    The meeting was held October 15, 2013, in the penthouse of the apartment building. (Two commas are needed for the additional part.)

    NOTE: Many writers remember to put in the first comma but forget the second one.

    The meeting was held Tuesday, October 15, 2013, in the penthouse of the apartment building. (Three commas are needed for the two additional parts.)

    The meeting was held October 2013 in the penthouse of the apartment building. (No comma is needed for a date with two parts.)

13. Addresses having more than one part require commas for each additional part except between the state and the zip code.

> The package addressed to Ms. Liza Barrows, 200 Main Street, York, PA 17406, should be sent tomorrow.

> Christie is moving from Dagsboro, Delaware, to Los Angeles, California, at the end of the year.

NOTE: Many writers remember to put in the first comma between the city and the state, but forget the second one.

14. A comma is required prior to a quotation after the signal verb. If the quotation is split into two parts, two commas are used.

> Blair said, "Procrastination can be the key to flexibility."

> "Marriage is love," Tom declared, "and like and tolerate."

NOTE: Commas and periods go inside quotation marks.

EXERCISE 9.3

Choose the sentence that has no punctuation errors.

1. A. Birthdays are fun to celebrate, but, they don't always come on a convenient day of the year.
   B. Birthdays are fun to celebrate, but they don't always come on a convenient day of the year.
   C. Birthdays are fun to celebrate but, they don't always come on a convenient day of the year.

2. A. If you have a birthday on July 4 for instance your celebration competes with America's.
   B. If you have a birthday on July 4, for instance your celebration competes with America's.
   C. If you have a birthday on July 4, for instance, your celebration competes with America's.

3. A. Jane, who lives in my neighborhood, likes having her birthday on July 4 because she loves fireworks.
   B. Jane who lives in my neighborhood likes having her birthday on July 4 because she loves fireworks.
   C. Jane, who lives in my neighborhood, likes having her birthday on July 4, because she loves fireworks.

4. A. I realized that Baltimore, Maryland is a summer destination for many tourists.
   B. I realized that Baltimore Maryland, is a summer destination for many tourists.
   C. I realized that Baltimore, Maryland, is a summer destination for many tourists.

5. A. "If you file an extension for your tax return" said my accountant, "you still have to send in what you owe."

   B. "If you file an extension for your tax return", said my accountant, "you still have to send in what you owe."

   C. "If you file an extension for your tax return," said my accountant, "you still have to send in what you owe."

6. A. Yes Barry, I will buy you asparagus, scallions, and eggs at the farmers' market this morning.

   B. Yes, Barry, I will buy you asparagus, scallions, and eggs at the farmers' market this morning.

   C. Yes Barry, I will buy you asparagus, scallions and eggs at the farmers' market this morning.

7. A. Many people don't realize that there is a word for the next to last one, *penultimate*.

   B. Many people don't realize, that there is a word for the next to last one, *penultimate*.

   C. Many people don't realize that there is a word for the next to last one *penultimate*.

8. A. In Morris County New Jersey, first-time offenders can enter the Sheriff's Labor Assistance Program, or S.L.A.P.

   B. In Morris County New Jersey, first-time offenders can enter the Sheriff's Labor Assistance Program or S.L.A.P.

   C. In Morris County, New Jersey, first-time offenders can enter the Sheriff's Labor Assistance Program or S.L.A.P.

9. A. First-time offenders, usually young people, can help the county by picking up trash from the roadways, weeding gardens at local parks and trimming bushes and trees.

   B. First-time offenders, usually young people, can help the county by picking up trash from the roadways, weeding gardens at local parks, and trimming bushes and trees.

   C. First-time offenders usually young people can help the county by picking up trash from the roadways, weeding gardens at local parks, and trimming bushes and trees.

10. A. In return for their hard work, their record is wiped clean as if they were never guilty of a crime.

    B. In return for their hard work, their record is wiped clean, as if they were never guilty of a crime.

    C. In return for their hard work their record is wiped clean as if they were never guilty of a crime.

EXERCISE 9.4

Clearly insert commas where they are needed. Write "Correct" next to sentences with correct punctuation.

1. YouTube a video-sharing website was created by three friends Chad Hurley Steve Chen and Jawed Karim who all worked together at PayPal.

2. On April 23 2014 YouTube marked nine years since its first video was posted a video titled "Me at the Zoo" showing co-founder Jared Karim at the San Diego Zoo.

3. Google bought YouTube in November 2006 for $1.65 billion and Hurley Chen and Karim became very wealthy young men.

4. Users can upload view and share videos and registered users can upload as many videos as they want.

5. Most of the content on YouTube is uploaded by individuals but some corporations like Hulu the BBC and CBS have partnerships with the website.

6. YouTube is not just comprised of raunchy music videos and silly amateur videos of people doing stupid stunts; as a matter of fact YouTube is quickly becoming the front-runner for educational videos.

7. Despite its educational uses YouTube is under scrutiny in other countries for example Saudi Arabia.

8. Many American don't realize that Saudi Arabia is one of the biggest per-capita consumers of YouTube because of its large population of young people.

9. The government-backed media in Saudi Arabia does not produce enough content that young people crave like news satire and comedy.

10. If the conservative Islamic kingdom starts to scrutinize the content of YouTube the creators of that content could have their creativity suppressed.

CHAPTER 10
Confidence

Photo courtesy of James G. and Elizabeth R. Troutman

PERSUASION—PROPOSING A SOLUTION

In the last chapter, you worked on taking a position on an issue. A similar type of persuasive writing involves making a proposal claim, proposing a solution to a problem. This type of claim involves two ideas: (1) determining that a problem exists and convincing readers that it does, and (2) identifying and explaining a reasonable solution to the problem. These types of claims often take the position that something should or should not be done.

Persuasive writing requires the writer to do much convincing of the reader. In writing a proposal paper, you have four aims:

1. You must convince the reader that there is indeed a problem.

2. You must convince the reader that your solution is better than other solutions. The other solutions are part of your opposing viewpoints.

3. You must convince the reader that there will be benefits in solving the problem.

4. You must convince the reader to take action if you are proposing that the reader directly do something about the problem.

A proposal paper can make a claim that something should or should not be done, and this solution will be carried out by someone other than the reader. Or, a proposal paper can include the reader in the solution. This second type of proposal is making a direct claim to the reader to do something about the problem that you present. The assumption has to be made in this second type that your reader has some sort of authority and connection to the problem in order to be part of its solution.

Consideration of your reader, once again, is a foremost concern in this type of writing. You have to know where your readers stand in order to move them in the direction that you want them to. If your readers are your professor and classmates, then you have a small audience, but it is still a diverse one. You should consider that they have a certain level of doubt about the claim you are making. A slightly doubtful or biased audience is one that will give you the energy that is required of persuasive writing. If your readers totally agree with you then there is no need for you to persuade them. However, in a proposal paper, you have many opportunities to raise disagreement in your readers' minds. They might consider what you perceive to be a problem, not a problem at all. Or, they might think another solution is better than the one you propose. Or, they might find your solution impractical.

You must search your own thoughts in order to find a problem that's worth solving and that can be solved. Generally, time and space constraints will cause you to choose a relatively small problem that affects a small group of people. Or, if indeed the problem is shared by many people, then how can it be changed or solved at just a local level?

Finally, you must support your proposal with good reasons for your solution. These reasons are generally the same as the benefits of your solution. And, depending on your audience, your readers might benefit directly.

Prompt 10.1

The general topic for this double-spaced, two paged essay is a problem that a student might have in his or her first semester of college and its solution. You will have to create a more focused, specific topic.

Your objective for this essay is to decide on a specific problem that a student might encounter in his or her first semester of college. This can be a problem you had (or have) or one that a friend had (or is still having). You will have to describe the problem in detail. You also need to consider why the problem is indeed a problem.

You will also have to explore solutions. You should discuss what goals must be served by whatever action or solution is taken. You should consider the consequences of each possible action or solution.

Finally, you will need to investigate the best possible solution to the problem. You should be prepared to address the following questions:

> Which course of action is the best?
>
> How will the solution solve the problem?
>
> What will be achieved in solving the problem?

All paragraphs will explain, illustrate, and discuss your specific topic with clarity, unity, coherence, and detail. Consider that your essay will be published in a collection of essays for next year's freshman class and their parents. The title of the publication could be *Problems First-Year College Students Encounter and Their Solutions*. Your current classmates and professors will also read this collection.

You might decide to have your thesis statement be your best solution to the problem. In this way, your essay will address why other solutions will not work as well as yours. Additionally, you will have to supply reasons for why your solution is an effective one.

Prompt 10.2

Make a list of all the things you find annoying on your college campus. This list should include policies and programs that exist and are not working, so they need to be changed or discontinued. You should also include things that you find annoying because they are not available, so they should be made available. Then, review your list to find something that other students are annoyed by as well. Consult with other students to ensure that you are not alone in your opinions. Think about what change should occur to eliminate the annoyance, or at the very least, make the annoyance less of one.

Write a letter to your college administration, proposing the change be implemented. First, you will have to persuade the administration that this issue is important to you and other students. Then, you have to persuade the readers how this situation can be better for not just you, but other students as well. You should think how this situation is justifiably an annoyance and how your recommendation is a good one that will be taken seriously by the college's administration.

You will want to give particular attention to your tone for this prompt. You should strive for a reasonable, respectful tone that shows you have the ethos, the credibility, and sincerity, to be taken seriously by your reader.

ANALYZING A PROPOSAL CLAIM

It's always helpful to read others' persuasive writing so that our own will be improved. While you have been thinking about problems and solutions that affect you on a more local level, other issues affect larger communities that you are a part of.

Most Americans have opinions about problems with stereotyping, whether by gender, race, religion, or any other part of our identities. What follows is an examination of the country's reaction to the unfortunate death of Trayvon Martin, a seventeen-year-old high school student, who was shot and killed by George Zimmerman on the night of February 26, 2012. Zimmerman was a neighborhood watch coordinator in Sanford, Florida, where Trayvon was living and where the shooting took place.

Prompt 10.3

Before reading President Barack Obama's speech that he made after a Florida jury acquitted George Zimmerman of second-degree murder and manslaughter charges for the death of Trayvon Martin, write two to three paragraphs about what you know already surrounding the death of Trayvon Martin in Sanford, Florida.

THE DEATH OF TRAYVON MARTIN

On July 13, 2013, a Florida jury acquitted George Zimmerman of second-degree murder and manslaughter charges. President Barack Obama made the following speech at the White House on July 19, 2013.

THE DEATH OF TRAYVON MARTIN

"The reason I actually wanted to come out today is not to take questions, but to speak to an issue that obviously has gotten a lot of attention over the course of the last week–the issue of the Trayvon Martin ruling. I gave a preliminary statement right after the ruling on Sunday. But watching the debate over the course of the last week, I thought it might be useful for me to expand on my thoughts a little bit." 1

"First of all, I want to make sure that, once again, I send my thoughts and prayers, as well as Michelle's, to the family of Trayvon Martin, and to remark on the incredible grace and dignity with which they've dealt with the entire situation. I can only imagine what they're going through, and it's remarkable how they've handled it." 2

"The second thing I want to say is to reiterate what I said on Sunday, which is there's going to be a lot of arguments about the legal issues in the case. I'll let all the legal analysts and talking heads address those issues. The judge conducted the trial in a professional manner. The prosecution and the defense made their arguments. The juries were properly instructed that in a case such as this reasonable doubt was relevant, and they rendered a verdict. And once the jury has spoken, that's how our system works. But I did want to just talk a little bit about context and how people have responded to it and how people are feeling." 3

"You know, when Trayvon Martin was first shot I said that this could have been my son. Another way of saying that is Trayvon Martin could have been me thirty-five years ago. And when 4 you think about why, in the African American community at least, there's a lot of pain around what happened here, I think it's important to recognize that the African American community is looking at this issue through a set of experiences and a history that doesn't go away."

"There are very few African American men in this country who haven't had the experience of being followed when they were shopping in a department store. That includes me. There are very few African American men who haven't had the experience of walking across the street and hearing the locks click on the doors of cars. That happens to me—at least before I was a senator. There are very few African Americans who haven't had the experience of getting on an elevator and a woman clutching her purse nervously and holding her breath until she had a chance to get off. That happens often."   5

"And I don't want to exaggerate this, but those sets of experiences inform how the African American community interprets what happened one night in Florida. And it's inescapable for people to bring those experiences to bear. The African American community is also knowledgeable that there is a history of racial disparities in the application of our criminal laws–everything from the death penalty to enforcement of our drug laws. And that ends up having an impact in terms of how people interpret the case."   6

"Now, this isn't to say that the African American community is naïve about the fact that African American young men are disproportionately involved in the criminal justice system; that they're disproportionately both victims and perpetrators of violence. It's not to make excuses for that fact—although black folks do interpret the reasons for that in a historical context. They understand that some of the violence that takes place in poor black neighborhoods around the country is born out of a very violent past in this country, and that the poverty and dysfunction that we see in those communities can be traced to a very difficult history."   7

"And so the fact that sometimes that's unacknowledged adds to the frustration. And the fact that a lot of African American boys are painted with a broad brush and the excuse is given, well, there are these statistics out there that show that African American boys are more violent–using that as an excuse to then see sons treated differently causes pain."   8

"I think the African American community is also not naïve in understanding that, statistically, somebody like Trayvon Martin was statistically more likely to be shot by a peer than he was by somebody else. So folks understand the challenges that exist for African American boys. But they get frustrated I think, if they feel that there's no context for it and that context is being denied. And that all contributes I think to a sense that if a white male teen was involved in the same kind of scenario, that from top to bottom, both the outcome and the aftermath might have been different."   9

"Now, the question for me at least, and I think for a lot of folks, is where do we take this? How do we learn some lessons from this and move in a positive direction? I think it's understandable that there have been demonstrations and vigils and protests, and some of that stuff is just going to have to work its way through, as long as it remains nonviolent. If I see any violence, then I will remind folks that that dishonors what happened to Trayvon Martin and his family. But beyond protests or vigils, the question is, are there some concrete things that we might be able to do."   10

"I know that Eric Holder[1] is reviewing what happened down there, but I think it's important for people to have some clear expectations here. Traditionally, these are issues of state and local government, the criminal code. And law enforcement is traditionally done at the state and local levels, not at the federal levels."   11

---

1. Eric Holder is the first African American to have the position of U.S. Attorney General. He has served in President Barack Obama's administration since 2009.

"That doesn't mean, though, that as a nation we can't do some things that I think would be productive. So let me just give a couple of specifics that I'm still bouncing around with my staff, so we're not rolling out some five-point plan, but some areas where I think all of us could potentially focus." 12

"Number one, precisely because law enforcement is often determined at the state and local level, I think it would be productive for the Justice Department, governors, mayors to work with law enforcement about training at the state and local levels in order to reduce the kind of mistrust in the system that sometimes currently exists." 13

"When I was in Illinois, I passed racial profiling legislation, and it actually did just two simple things. One, it collected data on traffic stops and the race of the person who was stopped. But the other thing was it resourced us training police departments across the state on how to think about potential racial bias and ways to further professionalize what they were doing." 14

"And initially, the police departments across the state were resistant, but actually they came to recognize that if it was done in a fair, straightforward way that it would allow them to do their jobs better and communities would have more confidence in them and, in turn, be more helpful in applying the law. And obviously, law enforcement has got a very tough job." 15

"So that's one area where I think there are a lot of resources and best practices that could be brought to bear if state and local governments are receptive. And I think a lot of them would be. And let's figure out are there ways for us to push out that kind of training[?]" 16

"Along the same lines, I think it would be useful for us to examine some state and local laws to see if it—if they are designed in such a way that they may encourage the kinds of altercations and confrontations and tragedies that we saw in the Florida case, rather than diffuse potential altercations." 17

"I know that there's been commentary about the fact that the Stand Your Ground[2] laws in Florida were not used as a defense in the case. On the other hand, if we're sending a message as a society in our communities that someone who is armed potentially has the right to use those firearms even if there's a way for them to exit from a situation, is that really going to be contributing to the kind of peace and security and order that we'd like to see?" 18

"And for those who resist that idea that we should think about something like these Stand Your Ground laws, I'd just ask people to consider, if Trayvon Martin was of age and armed, could he have stood his ground on that sidewalk? And do we actually think that he would have been justified in shooting Mr. Zimmerman who had followed him in a car because he felt threatened? And if the answer to that question is at least ambiguous, then it seems to me that we might want to examine those kinds of laws." 19

"Number three—and this is a long-term project–we need to spend some time in thinking about how do we bolster and reinforce our African American boys. And this is something that Michelle and I talk a lot about. There are a lot of kids out there who need help who are getting a lot of negative reinforcement. And is there more that we can do to give them the sense that their country cares about them and values them and is willing to invest in them?" 20

"I'm not naïve about the prospects of some grand, new federal program. I'm not sure that that's what we're talking about here. But I do recognize that as president, I've got some convening power, and there are a lot of good programs that are being done across the country on this front. And for us to be able to gather together business leaders and local elected officials and clergy and celebrities and athletes, and figure out how are we doing a better job helping young African American men feel that they're a full part of this society and that they've got pathways and 21

---

2. Florida has this law that permits a person to use deadly force in an act of self-defense.

avenues to succeed–I think that would be a pretty good outcome from what was obviously a tragic situation. And we're going to spend some time working on that and thinking about that."

"And then, finally, I think it's going to be important for all of us to do some soul-searching. 22 There has been talk about [whether we] should convene a conversation on race. I haven't seen that [to] be particularly productive when politicians try to organize conversations. They end up being stilted and politicized, and folks are locked into the positions they already have. On the other hand, in families and churches and workplaces, there's the possibility that people are a little bit more honest, and at least you ask yourself your own questions about, am I wringing as much bias out of myself as I can? Am I judging people as much as I can based on not the color of their skin, but the content of their character? That would, I think, be an appropriate exercise in the wake of this tragedy."

"And let me just leave you with a final thought that, as difficult and challenging as this whole 23 episode has been for a lot of people, I don't want us to lose sight that things are getting better. Each successive generation seems to be making progress in changing attitudes when it comes to race. It doesn't mean we're in a post-racial society. It doesn't mean that racism is eliminated. But when I talk to Malia and Sasha[3], and I listen to their friends and I see them interact, they're better than we are–they're better than we were on these issues. And that's true in every community that I've visited all across the country."

"And so we have to be vigilant and we have to work on these issues. And those of us in author- 24 ity should be doing everything we can to encourage the better angels of our nature, as opposed to using these episodes to heighten divisions. But we should also have confidence that kids these days, I think, have more sense than we did back then, and certainly more than our parents did or our grandparents did; and that along this long, difficult journey, we're becoming a more perfect union–a perfect union, but a more perfect union."

---

3. Malia and Sasha are President Barack Obama and Michelle Obama's daughters. Malia was born on July 4, 1998, and Sasha was born June 10, 2001.

Reaction to Writing

1. If you do not know the meanings of the following words, try to determine their meaning from the surrounding context in President Obama's speech. Check their meanings in a dictionary and write a sentence using each word.

   reiterate (3)

   disparities (6)

   naïve (7)

   dysfunction (7)

   concrete (10)

   altercations (17)

ambiguous (19)

convening (21)

stilted (22)

wringing (22)

wake (22)

2. How would this speech be different if President Obama was not African American?

3. Given that a jury found George Zimmerman not guilty, what specifically is the problem that President Obama is addressing?

4. What are the four solutions or changes that President Obama proposes?

Prompt 10.4

Choose one of the solutions that President Obama proposes that you provided as the answer for question number four above. Write a short essay of at least three paragraphs evaluating and expanding upon the solution. How would the solution work? Has the solution been tried elsewhere in perhaps a different context? If so, what outcomes have been reached? What are the limitations of the solution?

APOSTROPHES

Apostrophes cause writers so many problems. In fact, some people think that the apostrophe should be banished altogether. Regardless of the unlikelihood of the disappearance of apostrophes, they do serve a few purposes. Apostrophes are used to show possession or ownership of nouns and indefinite pronouns and to show time and measurement. They are also used to show the omissions of letters as in the case of contractions, and they are used to make letters plural.

Two common errors with apostrophes happen when they are used to make nouns plural and when they are used in possessive pronouns. And, once again, computer software programs like grammar-check are quite weak when it comes to helping writers use apostrophes.

NO: The developer built the ten house's so close together. (An apostrophe is not used to make the noun *house* plural.)

YES: The developer built the ten houses so close together.

NO: America has a challenge with repairing all of it's dilapidated bridges. (*It's* is the contraction for *it is*, not the possessive pronoun *its*.)

YES: America has a challenge with repairing all of its dilapidated bridges.

Apostrophes Used to Show Possession of Nouns and Indefinite Pronouns

○ When a noun does not end with an *s*, you add *'s* to show possession.

- The writer's keyboard is broken.
- Jill's new carpeting is so soft.
- The children's toys are all over the living room.

○ When a singular noun ends with an *s*, you add *'s* to show possession.

- The bus's tires had to be replaced.
- James's sailboat is now in the water for the summer season.

○ When a plural noun ends with an *s*, you add only an apostrophe to show possession.

- The five books' covers were missing.
- The oak trees' leaves are almost all down.

○ Add *'s* to show possession for an indefinite pronoun. Consult Table 7.1 for a list of indefinite pronouns.

- Everyone's presents are under the Christmas tree.
- Somebody's umbrella is in my car.

Apostrophes Used to Show Measurement and Time

Apostrophes are used in expressions that indicate measurement or time. The same rules from above apply here.

> Matt gave his employer one month's notice.
>
> Most companies offer at least four weeks' maternity leave to their employees.

Apostrophes Used in Contractions

Always check with your professors to find out if using contractions is allowed for their specific course and subject. Contractions are becoming more acceptable in academic writing, but my advice is to avoid overusing them. Some professors still find them unacceptable in formal writing.

An apostrophe stands in for the missing letter or letters in contractions.

> She isn't aware of any problems. = She is not aware of any problems.
>
> Let's have dinner later tonight. = Let us have dinner later tonight.

Box 10.1 lists the common contractions.

One contraction that is always allowed is for the expression *o'clock* as in time. Apostrophes also stand in for missing numbers.

> The '80s were good years for rock and roll. (The apostrophe is standing in for 19 as in the 1980s.)

BOX 10.1

Common Contractions

aren't = are not	isn't = is not	we're = we are
can't = cannot	it's = it is	weren't = were not
couldn't = could not	let's = let us	we've = we have
didn't = did not	she'd = she would, she had	who'd = who would, who had
don't = do not	she'll = she will	who'll = who will
he'd = he would, he had	she's = she is	who's = who is, who has
he'll = he will	there's = there is	won't = will not
he's = he is, he has	they'd = they would, they had	wouldn't = would not
I'd = I would, I had	they'll = they will	you'd = you would, you had
I'll = I will	they're = they are	you'll = you will
I'm = I am	they've = they have	you're = you are
I've = I have	wasn't = was not	you've = you have

Apostrophes Used to Make Letters Plural

The **only** time that an apostrophe is used to make something plural is in the case of letters.

Make sure your t's are crossed and your i's are dotted.

For letters that are acronyms, such as the SAT for the Scholastic Aptitude Test, only an *s* is added to make the acronym plural.

Taking the SATs can be stressful for teenagers.

EXERCISE 10.1

Circle or underline the correct choice.

One (month / months / month's) time is not long enough for college (students / students') to question if they made the right decision to go to college. No one should consider dropping out of college at this point. (Students / Students') have many ideas about their future plans. They probably have (friends / friends') who decided not to go to college. These (friends / friends') could be adding (pressures / pressure's) for a college student to drop out of college and return home. Then, everything will be the same as it was in high school.

(Teenagers / Teenagers') minds seem to be made up by the end of their senior year in high school. With the excitement of (proms / proms') and graduation, soon-to-be college (students / students') think about what (others / other's) are doing with their future. They listen to (other's / others / others') ideas and compare them to their own. Their (parents / parents') advice is also fairly important in (decisions / decisions') about leaving home for college.

Homesickness can set in during less than one (semester / semesters / semester's) time. Seeing the (colleges / college's / colleges') counselors can help (students / students') cope with homesickness and any other problems they could be having while adjusting to college. (Everyone's / Everyones) ideas are important to a college (student / student's) future. Decisions can be made after students consider all of their (options /

options'). Trying another semester or looking at other (schools / schools') is always a possibility. Students

should know that they do not have to be alone with their (decisions / decisions').

EXERCISE 10.2

Insert necessary apostrophes and/or the letter "s" in the following sentences. In the space provided for each sentence, write the corrected word. If none were corrected, write "Correct."

1. _____ In five years time, Liz hopes to have saved enough money to buy her first home.

2. _____ If you take the elevator to the fourth floor, you will find Dr. Gibsons office.

3. _____ In a little over a years time, Andrea was able to finish her double major requirements.

4. _____ That graduate assistant position requires at least two years tutoring experience in the writing center.

5. _____ Some of their credit card balances were forgiven; therefore, the couples credit history improved.

6. _____ Many defendants believe that lie-detector tests are not admissible evidence.

7. _____ Many of our alumni members phone numbers and e-mail addresses must be collected.

8. _____ The manager frequently had to check Dennis business statements.

9. _____ Josh believes that this stores prices are much better than the other stores.

10. _____ After paying four years tuition, he had no student loans.

11. _____ The Smiths daughter was leaving for Georgia at the end of the month.

12. _____ Mr. Jones thinks that he spent a years savings to put his son in rehab.

13. _____ The lease is not finalized without Ms. James signature.

14. _____ The new waiters table was the only one available.

15. _____ Alex dreams include finding a satisfying career and having a large family.

16. _____ In two months, three restaurants opening nights will occur in the town of Pittsville.

17. _____ My friend Mike still buys all of his DVDs rather than renting them.

18. _____ I always get my moneys worth at my favorite restaurant.

CONCISENESS AND CLARITY

Despite what you might think or what you might have learned, writing more is not always writing better. Wordiness is the opposite of conciseness. Direct, concise writing is valued in college as well as in the workplace. You probably are not happy to hear that wordiness is generally not rewarded. It doesn't seem quite fair that so many teachers require a word count in their writing assignments, yet you aren't supposed to pad your writing with extra words. However, your good thinking comes across more clearly when your writing is concise.

   2L2R   =   Too long to read

Wordy Expressions

When we use wordy expressions, we might be trying to make our writing sound more important or educated. But, we might also just be using them out of habit. The following list has some of these wordy expressions with their concise replacements. Review this list and mark the expressions that you use in your writing, causing wordiness.

Instead of this…	Try this…
because of the fact that	because
due to the fact that	because
despite the fact that	although
in spite of the fact that	although
in addition to	also
in all probability	probably
we are of the opinion	we think
it is believed by many	many believe
have a tendency to	tends to
in order to	to
for the purpose of	to
at this point in time	now
at the present time	now
at a later date/time	later
for the period of	for
in the event that	if

Instead of this…	Try this…
in the untimely event that	if
in the near future	soon
making an effort to	trying to
in very few cases	seldom
in a thoughtful manner	thoughtfully
in a careful manner	carefully

One other construction that is wordy and redundant is *the reason is because* and *the reason why* or *the reason why is because*.

NO: The reason toddlers might wander away from their parents is because of a new sense of independence.

YES: Toddlers might wander away from their parents because of a new sense of independence.

Empty Sentence Starters

The sentence starters *there is/was*, *there are/were*, and *it is/was* create wordiness also. These sentence starters delay the real subject of the sentence. In many instances, writers can revise their sentences to eliminate these wordy starters, but sometimes they are necessary for coherence and emphasis.

NO: There are many solutions to the problem.

YES: Many solutions to the problem exist.

NO: There is only one student signed up for writing center tutoring tonight.

YES: Only one student signed up for writing center tutoring tonight.

NO: It was the baseball player who protected the fan.

YES: The baseball player protected the fan.

Using Gargantuan (Big) Words

I used the word *gargantuan* in the above heading to emphasize my point regarding word choice. Sometimes writers use big words in order to sound more important or educated. I see examples of unnaturally enlarged words in my students' writing all the time. While a thesaurus can be useful when you are looking for a more precise word, be wary of using one when you are simply looking for a big word to sound smarter. Rarely does the bigger word have the intended meaning of the simpler, more precise word.

NO: I feel repugnance toward her.

YES: I dislike her.

NO: It causes me great vexation.

YES: It bothers me.

NO: The movie's ending is a rapturous one.

YES: The movie's ending is happy.

Making Nouns from Verbs

Another source of wordiness is the practice of making nouns from verbs. This happens when the endings *–tion*, *-ment*, and *–ance* are added to verbs, turning them into nouns and wordy noun phrases. When writers turn wordy noun phrases back into stronger verbs, their writing becomes more concise.

> NO: We will begin an investigation.
>
> YES: We will investigate.
>
> NO: They are in full agreement
>
> YES: They fully agree.
>
> NO: The proposal had the acceptance of all.
>
> YES: Everyone accepted the proposal.

EXERCISE 10.3

Revise the following sentences to eliminate wordiness. Look for wordy expressions, empty sentence starters, unnaturally enlarged words, and wordy noun phrases made out of verbs.

1. At this point in time, the apartment building had the appearance of being empty.

2. He has the tendency to have a resistance to caffeine.

3. There is a preponderance of students who have a reliance on Wikipedia.

4. The reason senior citizens might drive more slowly than younger drivers is due to the fact that they have impairment of eyesight and reaction time.

5. It is believed by many that the existence of aliens is real.

6. Susan made the decision to change jobs in spite of the fact that the new job had a longer commute.

7. It is my intention to put in a request for a transfer in the near future.

8. The reason why men have a preference for long hair on women is because they like to touch it.

9. Jake gave the matter his consideration in a thoughtful manner.

10. The child was unable to complete the construction of the toy due to the fact that a piece was missing.

EVALUATING YOUR PERSUASIVE ESSAY

When you are finished drafting a persuasive essay, the following information should be helpful when you start revising.

Introduction

First, you must make sure that your essay is only discussing one single issue.

- ○ Have I focused on one single issue in my essay? Does my essay have unity?
- ○ Does my introduction clearly set forth my thesis?

Every introduction has two essential functions: It must *inform* the readers about the subject, and it must *interest* them enough to make them want to read further.

- ○ Does my introduction make my readers want to read further?

In your introduction, you must find something new and important to say, find a simpler way to discuss something often considered complex, or describe a vivid example to raise your readers' interest.

Background Information

At some point, often after the introduction, but sometimes as part of it, you may need to provide background information about your subject, defining key terms, and giving enough information so that your readers will understand the subject correctly.

- ○ What have I left undefined?
- ○ Have I taken for granted anything the reader might not readily understand or accept?

Support

This is the core of your essay: the reasons, examples, and evidence you offer in support of your thesis.

- ○ What have I left unsupported?
- ○ Where have I failed to be concrete when I might have given specific examples?

Organize your points clearly and logically. No magic formula for organizing points exists; just be sure you have a rationale for the ordering that makes sense and enables you to move easily and naturally from one point to the next. While revising, keep in the mind the analogy of relay race strategy: end with the strongest runner, and don't begin with the weakest.

Opposing Viewpoints

You must always consider other possible ideas and viewpoints about the subject besides your own. To show that you have done so enhances your ethos substantially by demonstrating that you are both well informed and reasonable.

- ○ Have I considered all the possible dimensions of the problem, or all its possible solutions?
- ○ Have I made the necessary acknowledgments in regards to the opposing viewpoints?

Where you bring in opposing viewpoints depends on two factors: the nature of the issue and your sense of your audience. If the issue is controversial, mention the opposing viewpoints early on in the essay because they will be on the readers' minds anyway. If your subject is relatively complex, you may find it works best to alternate between making your own points and challenging opposing points.

Conclusion

The conclusion can be the most difficult part of an essay to write.

- ○ What idea am I trying to persuade my audience to accept?
- ○ How can I best emphasize or reassert my original thesis without repeating it?

If you don't ask these questions, you may be tempted to just stop, rather than conclude. When that happens, the essay either drops off abruptly, or mindlessly repeats what the readers have already been told. Consider a few other pointers: the rhetorical (open-ended) question—my own favorite type of conclusion during my high school years—grows tiresome with overuse. Second, a concluding quotation can be effective, but might weaken the power of your own persona. Usually you will do best to end in your own words.

CHAPTER 11

Discovery

Photo courtesy of James G. and Elizabeth R. Troutman

PERSUASION—EVALUATING AN ISSUE

In Chapter 9, we looked at persuasive writing, specifically used for taking a position on an issue. And, in Chapter 6, we covered writing evaluations or making judgments. When writers make evaluative claims, they are combining these two methods and putting forth a claim that makes a value judgment about a controversial issue to an audience who might not totally agree with them. You should remember in Chapter 6 we covered making simple evaluative claims that something is good or bad based off of generally accepted standards. Evaluating an issue requires persuasion when one or more of the following is part of the writing situation:

The issue that you are evaluating is controversial to your readers.

Your evaluative claim is debatable among your readers.

The standards that you use for your evaluative claim are less obvious to your readers.

Evaluating issues relies heavily on ethical considerations like social norms, values, morals, and behavioral standards. Because of these ethical considerations, this kind of persuasive writing requires a heightened sense of your audience. An evaluation like, for example, a movie review, relies on artistic considerations that are usually accepted by a general audience. These considerations would include standards like characters, plot, cinematography, and dialogue. Persuasion comes into the picture when the standards for an evaluation are less obvious.

A Student's Essay

In my fall 2013 persuasive writing class, I gave my students the assignment of writing an evaluation essay to an audience of their peers. Joncara Marshall wrote the following first and final drafts.

Joncara was born in Milford, Delaware, and has lived there all of her life. She likes nature, traveling, drawing, writing, books, movies, and animation (not creating it, but watching animated movies and television shows). Joncara graduated from Wesley College in Dover, Delaware, in May 2014, with an English degree. Next, she hopes to receive her Master's degree in journalism.

You will be able to see the comments that I provided Joncara when I gave her feedback on her first draft.

Marshall 1

Joncara Marshall

Dr. Shipley

EN211

November 30, 2013

First Draft- A World Made of Eggshells: How Men's Place in Society Is Affected by the

Patriarchal System

What is great about higher education is being exposed to all kinds of ideals and views

that you may not have heard before. However, one idea that you will be familiar with is how

female gender roles have changed. Without looking too far outside of your academic

environment, you can consider how women were not able to go to college or receive the same

type of education as men did. However, we sometimes forget that men have had a hard time in

society as well. I am not trying to diminish the historical significance of women's rights, but I do

think that students should keep in mind that men do not always have it easy in the society that

them ?

was created by men. Sometimes we do not think how men are sexualized and how they must live

the same as those for

up to a different set of expectations that are not necessarily expected from women. *women*

To be sexualized is to be seen as a something - an object-as opposed to as someone.

dashes not hyphens

Women have been objectified for centuries and, though it is not as bad as some generations

before ours, it is still prevalent in society. However, we sometimes do not consider how men are

also sexualized. In television, movies, magazines, and ads, men are also shown in provocative

strange wording

ways that, if they were women, would be seen as objectifying. Instead, I think, we deem

provocative images of men as normal, or, if it crosses some line, indecent.

- try to be more forceful
- do a search for the word "sometimes"

Marshall 2

In addition to be being sexualized, men also face a different set of expectations than women. A man must have a job, provide for his family, and be mature. Women, on the other hand, are not expected to do these things but rather strongly encouraged to do so. For example, it is not unusual, though not encouraged, to see a young woman still living with her parents until she is able to be independent. With men, they are expected to move out and be established, or at least able to take care of themselves by the age of 35 or maybe sooner.

vague [underlining "these things"]

need more examples

BE [caret]

EVEN [circled 5]

→ 35 ̂ seems too late

My argument is that a man's place in society should be considered, on both a personal and academic scale, by students. College is the best time to notice these changes as you will be in constant contact with someone who is of the opposite gender. In order to reach a sense of gender equality, we need to see how both men and women have changed over the course of time.

I'm not sure you've discovered your argument yet. You seem to want to evaluate a kind of double standard. Do more brainstorming to discover more expectations that are set for men. Your title seems to match what you're going for.

Reaction to Writing

1. What issue is Joncara evaluating?

2. What evaluative claim is Joncara making?

3. What standards for evaluation is Joncara using?

4. What other comments would you add to the ones I have on the first draft?

What follows is Joncara's final draft that she turned in for a grade.

Final Draft

Joncara Marshall

Dr. Shipley

EN211

December 12, 2013

Men Don't Have it Easy in a Patriarchal Society

What is great about higher education is being exposed to all kinds of ideas and views that you may not have heard before. However, one idea that you will be familiar with is how female gender roles have changed. Without looking too far outside of your academic environment, you can consider how women were not able to go to college or receive the same type of education as men did. However, we sometimes forget that men have had a hard time in society as well. I am not trying to diminish the historical significance of women's rights, but I do think that students should keep in mind that men do not always have it easy in the society that was created by them. Sometimes we do not think how men are sexualized and how they must live up to a different set of expectations that are not necessarily the same as those for women.

To be sexualized is to be seen as a "something"—an object—as opposed to "someone." Women have been objectified for centuries, and, though it is not as bad as some generations before ours, it is still prevalent in society. However, we do not consider how men are also sexualized. In television, movies, magazines, and ads, men are also shown in provocative ways that, if they were women, would be seen as offensive. Instead, we deem provocative images of men as normal, or, if

Marshall 2

it crosses some line, indecent. The problem of equalization, of both men and women, does not end but rather becomes a type of inequality that should not promoted.

In addition to be being sexualized, men also face a different set of expectations than women. For example, men are expected to have a job though they may not have a decent education; women, on the other hand, are pushed toward academia. In addition, it is not unusual, though not encouraged, to see a young woman still living with her parents until she is able to be independent. With men, they are expected to move out and be established, or at least, be able to take care of themselves by the age of twenty-five or maybe even sooner. These actions are due to the previous patriarchal system that has not died away and the strides that have been made to alter it; men are still expected to be the bread-winners, while women are encouraged to go above and beyond the boundaries that were placed on previous generations.

College is the best time to notice these changes as you will be in constant contact with someone who is of the opposite gender. In order to reach a sense of gender equality, we need to see how both men and women have changed over the course of time.

Reaction to Writing

1. What specifically did Joncara revise on her first draft to produce this final draft?

2. If Joncara had more time to produce yet another draft, what revisions would you suggest? Why?

3. What issues that you connect to does Joncara raise in her essay?

Prompt 11.1

Write a double-spaced, two to three paged essay joining the discussion that Joncara raises. Look at your answer to question number three above to get started. Your audience is the same as Joncara's, your peers. You are evaluating an issue within the broad issue of gender roles. You will have to narrow your focus considerably. Make your essay persuasive in that you consider opposing viewpoints.

CASTING STEREOTYPES

Probably no other issue raises more controversy than stereotyping. Stereotyping was an issue with the death of Trayvon Martin, wasn't it? Stereotypes are often false, and this generalizing of people can cause great damage. Unfortunately, we are all victims of stereotyping when we are stereotyped by others, and we are all guilty of stereotyping when we cast our assumptions about people. Casting is an interesting word here. It's used in fishing as in casting a line with a hook on the end of it, hoping the fish takes the bait. And that is exactly what we are doing when we cast stereotypes. We are throwing a judgment about a person or a group of people out there, hoping it will stick. Rarely does it.

President Obama referred to stereotyping when he said the following in his speech regarding the ruling of not guilty for George Zimmerman in the death of Trayvon Martin:

> "On the other hand, in families and churches and workplaces, there's the possibility that people are a little bit more honest, and at least you ask yourself your own questions about, am I wringing as much bias out of myself as I can? Am I judging people as much as I can, based on not the color of their skin, but the content of their character? That would, I think, be an appropriate exercise in the wake of this tragedy."

Of course, race is not the only part of our identities that is subject to stereotypes. Everything from our hair color to the way we speak is subject to scrutiny and often false generalizing.

EXERCISE 11.1

1. List important parts of your identity.

2. Consider stereotypes that you have heard about a part of your identity that you listed for question number one. List stereotypes that fail to describe you accurately.

3. How are parts of your identity different from the judgments that others make? Who are these "others" who are making these judgments?

4. How does this stereotype make you feel and others like you, maybe family members, feel?

5. How do you handle this stereotyping?

6. What stereotypes do you, your friends, and your family members have about other people?

Prompt 11.2

Using your work from Exercise 11.1, write a double-spaced, two to three paged essay about the ways in which you might have been stereotyped (based on where you live, how you speak, what you look like, and so on) and how you are like that stereotype and how you are not. Consider that your essay will be published in a collection of essays about stereotypes. Your classmates and your professors will read this collection.

Prompt 11.3

Using your work from Exercise 11.1, specifically question number six, write a double-spaced, two to three paged essay about the ways you or your family members or your friends stereotyped others. Discuss the consequences of casting stereotypes. Consider that your essay will be published in a collection of essays about stereotypes. Your classmates and your professors will read this collection.

A Student Example

The following essay about stereotyping is from a former student of mine. Due to the personal nature of her narrowed topic, I have not included her name.

Spics, Wetbacks, and Chalupas

When I was six years old, I came to the United States from Mexico with my parents and my older sister. Since then, my family worked hard to become legal citizens of America. Because I look Mexican, I have been stereotyped as an illegal immigrant all of my life. People should not group all Latinos into one category of being illegal immigrants.

It started in elementary school. I was constantly teased by the other kids for looking different and not being able to speak English very well. Young children often tease other kids for anything considered not "normal." However, their teasing and name calling made me hate school. Here I was at not only a new school but in a new country. I only wanted to fit in with the other kids and be accepted for me and not my looks and ethnicity.

Eventually, I learned to speak English as well, if not better, than Spanish. But as I entered my teenage years, the stereotypes became worse. I look, quite simply, Mexican. As I grew older, my body did not grow. I'm short, a little plump, with long dark hair, dark brown eyes, and a light brown complexion. I couldn't hide my looks. One time, I was driving in New Jersey, and I was pulled over by a police officer for no other reason, I believe, except that I look Mexican. The police officer asked if I had a driver's license. I just knew he thought I was probably an illegal immigrant. Of course, I was able to show him my driver's license to prove that I was legal. I drove away not knowing why he pulled me over in the first place.

Probably the worst situation so far in my life was the time when I was in the emergency room at the hospital because I needed stitches after cutting myself accidentally with a knife. A case worker came in to the little area where I was waiting and said to me directly, "I'm sure you don't have insurance since you are illegal, right?" I couldn't believe my ears. Fortunately, I was able to show her my insurance card, but it really didn't make the situation much better.

My family and I are Mexican Americans, and we are legal citizens of America. My father is a physician, and my mother is a florist who owns her own store. We work hard, we pay our taxes, and we obey all the laws. People stereotype us because they are ignorant to how immigration works in this country. The Mexicans who are in this country illegally are working jobs that American citizens do not want because the work is hard and the pay is low. All Americans should consider that people who look different actually add to this great country, and we are not a threat to anyone.

PERSUASION—EVALUATING AN ISSUE

Evaluating an issue requires persuasion when one or more of the following is part of the writing situation:

The issue that you are evaluating is controversial to your readers.

Your evaluative claim is debatable among your readers.

The standards that you use for your evaluative claim are less obvious to your readers.

In order to consider the many ways an issue can be evaluated, let's consider the comic strip *Doonesbury* by cartoonist Garry Trudeau. The following cartoon appeared in Sunday newspapers on October 27, 2013.

Reaction to Cartoon

1. The characters portrayed in this cartoon are from the fictional Walden College. What is the controversial issue being evaluated by Garry Trudeau?

2. Try to determine the meaning of *monetize* and *cohort* from the surrounding context. Check their meanings in a dictionary and write a sentence using each word.

3. Other than your answer for question number one, what other issues is Trudeau raising?

Prompt 11.4

Write a double-spaced, two to three paged persuasive essay with the broad topic of student-athletes in college. You will need to narrow this topic considerably. Consider all of the various attributes of persuasion that your writing might follow:

What will your position be about your narrowed topic?

Will you be proposing a solution or a change? If so, what will that solution or change look like?

Will you be evaluating an issue?

What are the opposing viewpoints?

How will you acknowledge these opposing viewpoints?

You should first interview at least two student-athletes, even if you are a student-athlete yourself. You should do this first as part of your brainstorming to help plan the shape that your persuasive writing will take.

As a reminder, make sure that you do not make generalizations. Consult Box 6.1 to review qualifying words. Your audience for this piece of writing is a broad one. Consider your readers to be the same readers of a newspaper like the *New York Times*. In other words, your readers are informed and interested in what college students have to say about this issue. Your readers also have a wide variety of opinions, so you will need to consider **all** sides of this issue and **all** viewpoints that are different than your own.

NOTE: I have struggled with my writing students about the terminology for college students who play intercollegiate sports and for those who do not. The best terms we have constructed are *student-athletes* for those who play intercollegiate sports and *non-athlete students* for those who do not.

COLONS, DASHES, AND OTHER PUNCTUATION

Colons

A colon is a form of punctuation that brings a reader to a full stop, similar to a period, at the end of an independent clause, a complete sentence. In other words, a sentence that is able to stand on its own must come before a colon. Four grammatical structures can follow a colon:

1. A complete sentence followed by a colon introduces a list.

   I have many reasons that make Friday my favorite day of the week: my weekly paycheck, happy hour with co-workers, and the upcoming weekend to look forward to.

2. A complete sentence followed by a colon introduces a quotation.

   My friend Blair has this wise advice for single men who are dating: "How do you know the true beauty of a rose without getting stuck by a thorn?"

3. A complete sentence followed by a colon introduces an appositive, a word or words that rename a noun or pronoun in the sentence prior to the colon.

   Our favorite football team has won the Super Bowl twice: the Baltimore Ravens. (The Baltimore Ravens renames our favorite football team.)

4. A complete sentence can be followed by a colon and another complete sentence that explains or summarizes the first sentence. In this instance, the colon acts like an equal (=) sign where the two complete sentences balance each other. The second sentence can start with a lowercase letter or a capital letter. Writers should be consistent throughout a piece of writing, either always using a lowercase letter to start the second sentence after a colon or always using a capital letter.

   The hurricane season is predicted to be below average this year: Forecasters think El Nino will diminish the number of hurricanes.

Writers create a usage error with a colon when they do not have a complete sentence prior to a colon. This frequently occurs with lead-in expressions that introduce examples: *including, such as, for example,* and *like*.

NO:	When she is grocery shopping, Susan always forgets the basics, such as: eggs, milk, bread, and toilet paper.
YES:	When she is grocery shopping, Susan always forgets the basics: eggs, milk, bread, and toilet paper.

Do not use a colon, unless you have a complete sentence prior to it.

NO:	For the cruise vacation, Ari was told: "Pack lightly."
YES:	For the cruise vacation, Ari was told, "Pack lightly."
NO:	The cabins on cruise ships do not have much room to store: lots of clothing and shoes, scuba gear, and electronic equipment.
YES:	The cabins on cruise ships do not have much room to store lots of clothing and shoes, scuba gear, and electronic equipment.
YES:	The cabins on cruise ships do not have much room to store many items: lots of clothing and shoes, scuba gear, and electronic equipment.

EXERCISE 11.2

Insert colons where needed and delete them where they are used incorrectly. Replace incorrectly used colons with commas if required. If a sentence is punctuated correctly, write "Correct."

1. Many animals in the wild have symbiotic relationships with other animals mutual relationships that support each other for survival.

2. For example, the African elephant has symbiotic relationships with other species baboons, antelopes, and birds.

3. When there are particularly dry conditions, elephants dig holes in the sand, producing drinking water in the holes for other thirsty animals, such as: baboons.

4. At the same time, baboons sit in the trees and can see approaching danger: they alert elephants with loud cries when they sense potential predators.

5. In 2003, eleven elephants rescued antelopes that were held in a Zululand conservation camp the Thula Thula Exclusive Private Game Reserve.

6. The head of the elephant herd somehow opened the camp's gate, allowing the antelopes to escape.

7. A Thula Thula scientist could not explain this behavior, stating: "Elephants are innately curious, but this rescue is highly unusual and cannot be explained scientifically."

8. Elephants have symbiotic relationships with birds including: cattle egrets and oxpeckers.

9. The birds ride along on the elephants' backs, where they eat pests from the elephants' skin ticks, lice, parasites, and other insects.

10. In this symbiotic relationship, the cattle egrets and oxpeckers get a free traveling meal the elephants get irritating pests and potentially harmful parasites removed.

11. In addition, the birds make loud screams when they notice: predators and other dangers nearby.

12. The elephants know the birds are watching out for them and their babies by making these warning alarms high-pitched screams often from the elephants' backs.

Dashes

The use of a dash or a pair of dashes is becoming more acceptable in academic writing. However, they should be used sparingly because they interrupt your writing and can create a jerking motion for your reader. You can create a dash by pressing the hyphen key twice (--). You should not have a space before the dash or after it. Many word processing programs will recognize two hyphens together and convert them to a dash. When you use a dash, it should appear as twice as long as a hyphen.

A dash or a pair of dashes signals special emphasis. Writers might want this special emphasis to show an example, an appositive, or a contrast. When using a dash or a pair of dashes, the sentence should be structurally correct if the dash and the words after it or the pair of dashes and the words between them were removed from the sentence.

Punctuation marks—the colon, semi-colon, and the comma—can be so confusing for writers.

The dashes and the words between them present an example for punctuation marks. The dashes and the words between them can be removed and the sentence is still structurally complete.

Punctuation marks can be so confusing for writers.

If a single dash introduces an example, an appositive, or a contrast at the end of the sentence, the sentence prior to the dash must be an independent clause or a complete sentence.

I finally found a career that I think I will find fulfilling—chemical engineering.

EXERCISE 11.3

Determine if dashes are used correctly in the following sentences. If the punctuation is correct in a sentence, write "Correct." If the punctuation is incorrect, revise the sentence to correct it.

1. Bullying doesn't just happen with children in schools, it happens—with adults in the workplace.

2. Employees are being mistreated—often by their bosses—on a daily basis.

3. The helplessness of an employee who is being bullied is the same if—not worse—as a child in elementary school.

4. Employees need their jobs and—the income that comes with—them in order to support themselves and their families.

5. Companies need to have anti-bullying policies in place—and enforce them.

6. But anti-bullying policies should be developed with employees as part of the process not—a top-down approach.

7. Workers—and this is key—should be able to think about what kind of behavior is acceptable and unacceptable in the workplace.

8. Bullying even occurs in—of all places—at the National Football League with big, tough football players.

9. Miami Dolphins lineman Jonathan Martin left the team, accusing teammate Richie Incognito of sending him racist and threatening text messages and e-mails—among other abusive things.

10. Unfortunately, in the workplace—people don't know when to step up—when bullying becomes unbearable.

Parentheses

Parentheses within writers' prose allow writers to insert information like dashes. However, unlike dashes which add emphasis, parentheses take away emphasis in writing. Readers often ignore parentheses and the words enclosed within them. This is why documentation styles like MLA use parentheses for citations. The parenthetical citation is added information that the reader doesn't necessarily need to read in order to understand the writing. Other than using parentheses for documentation styles, parentheses should be used sparingly in academic writing. If the information is important, it should be built into the writing and not hidden away, enclosed in parentheses.

Hyphens

Hyphens have a variety of uses for writers. They are used for hyphenation when a word has to be divided by its syllables at the end of a typed line. Hyphenation generally is not used in academic writing, but if it is required, most word processing programs will hyphenate correctly for you. If you are writing by hand or using a computer without a hyphenation program, you should consult a dictionary to know how to break the word into its syllables for correct hyphenation.

Hyphens are also used when you are spelling out the numbers, *twenty-one* through *ninety-nine*. This does not apply to multiples of ten, obviously, for example, *thirty*.

Hyphens are used with the following prefixes: *all-*, *ex-*, *quasi-*, *great-*, and *self-*.

My ex-wife and my great-grandmother went to an all-inclusive resort in Florida.

Be careful with the prefix *self-*. A hyphen is used only if *self-* is a prefix, not the root word.

NO: self-ish

YES: selfish, self-serving, self-reliant

When two or more words need to work together to modify a noun after them, a hyphen is also used. However, when the same two or more words are not modifying a noun that follows them, and they are standing on their own in a sentence, hyphens are not used.

Times are tough for middle-class Americans.
Times are tough for Americans in the middle class.
I sometimes babysit an eight-year-old boy.
I sometimes babysit a boy who is eight years old.

Some words can create confusion for readers because they have two different meanings and the same spellings. In this case, a hyphen is used after the prefix.

recreation (means an activity)   re-creation (means the act of creating again)
redress (means to set right)   re-dress (means to dress again)

Finally, if two of the same letters fall next to each other in a word, a hyphen is used to avoid confusion.

NO: antiintellectual   reemerge   coowners
YES: anti-intellectual   re-emerge   co-owners

PERSUASION – DEBATING AN ISSUE

A good debate of an issue has two approaches: counterargument and challenging an argument. When we write persuasively, we often use both. When you offer a counterargument to an argument that someone has made, you offer a whole new claim regarding the issue, addressing ideas that the original argument didn't cover. By largely ignoring the original argument, you are implying that yours is better.

When writers counterargue, they might acknowledge another's argument, but they often do not consider it in detail. It's important, however, that writers do not use counterargument as a way to avoid what another's argument is stating. This would be a dishonest maneuver, and often readers will see through it.

Counterargument is an effective approach if you feel an argument fails to address parts of the overall issue or even the overall issue itself. You can spend your energy creating a persuasive piece of writing that is stronger and more effective than the original argument.

When you take a challenging approach to an argument that someone has made, you show all the limitations of the original argument. You can challenge both the underlying assumptions that the original argument is making and the evidence or reasons the argument puts forth for its claim. This approach often mirrors the same structure of the original argument. You move from one point to the next showing how each point can be discredited. If you offer a claim of your own, then you are using a combination of the two approaches, which is quite common.

"Stickers Send Wrong Message"

We return to a newspaper to look at yet another issue. The following article "Stickers Send Wrong Message" was published in an editorial section entitled "How We See It" in *The Maryland Coast Dispatch*, a newspaper serving Ocean City, Maryland, and its surrounding coastal communities. This article was first published January 24, 2014.

STICKERS SEND WRONG MESSAGE

You can tell a lot about people by the stickers adorned to their vehicles. You can see which football team is the household favorite, how well the driver's child does in school, political, and religious beliefs and even where they live. On the latter note, a sticker we have a spotted in increasing and disturbing frequencies reads, "FU I Live Here." 1

This elitist attitude in an area dependent entirely on the fact it's a vacation destination is appalling. We understand there are times when tourists can be a tad difficult in the nerves for a variety of reasons, but it's a healthier approach to not dwell on that inevitability of living in a resort area and be thankful they come here in the first place. 2

Tourism means everything to this area and its associated impact trickles down to nearly every segment of society. In one way or another, every single household in this area benefits from the 3 fact people choose to vacation here and spend their disposable income in this region. Stickers like this stink of entitlement and an inability to see the big picture because they take for granted people will continue to vacation in a place where they are not welcomed by some.

To be certain, those sporting these stickers are in the minority. Most of us are aware nearly all local livelihoods weigh heavily on the outside our dollars coming into economy.   4

Let's take a look at some key data as proof. The top 10 employer list in Ocean City is led by the Harrison Group, a hotel and restaurant company based in Ocean City, at 900 employees, or 3.3 percent of the entire country work force. The top 10 employers in Ocean City employ 3,907 people in various capacities, or 14 percent of the entire country workforce, according to Ocean City's Comprehensive Financial Report. Ten year's ago, the city's top 10 employers represented 12 percent of the workforce, confirming Ocean City's importance in the marketplace is only increasing.   5

These jobs are vital and thousands of families are dependent on being employed. Without a viable tourism base, these jobs would not exist. Its importance cannot be understated. Even farmers benefit from tourists because without the inflated property value base that's driven by Ocean City's prime real estate, taxes would be much higher on the land they live off of and on.   6

While in a store recently selling these stickers ($2.99 apiece), we inquired why they would carry them and presented our rant. The answer was if it sells we carry it That's a myopic approach, and we certainly hope the demand for them subsides. It's the wrong message to send to the visitors who are so critical to the entire economy.   7

Reaction to Writing

1. If you do not know the meanings of the following words, try to determine their meaning from the surrounding context in the editorial. Check their meanings in the dictionary and write a sentence using each word.

   elitist (2)

   inevitability (2)

   viable (6)

   rant (7)

   myopic (7)

2. What message do the writers of this editorial think these stickers send?

3. What are some of the assumptions that the editors are making when they say that these stickers are sending this particular message?

4. What are other messages that these stickers could be sending?

5. In paragraph two, it is written, "tourists can be a tad difficult on the nerves for a variety of reasons." What are some of these reasons?

Prompt 11.5

Write a two-paged letter to the editor in response to this editorial. Consider your reasons for your position carefully. Remember that issues are rarely black and white. Try to operate in the gray area, using both the challenging approach and counterargument to debate the issue.

CPSIA information can be obtained at www.ICGtesting.com
Printed in the USA
BVOW09s1828070816

-458180BV00004B/11/P